NATIONAL PARK SERVICE REFORM

HEARING

BEFORE THE

SUBCOMMITTEE ON
NATIONAL PARKS, FORESTS AND PUBLIC LANDS

OF THE

COMMITTEE ON
NATURAL RESOURCES
HOUSE OF REPRESENTATIVES

ONE HUNDRED THIRD CONGRESS

SECOND SESSION

ON

H.R. 4533

TO PROMOTE ENTREPRENEURIAL MANAGEMENT OF THE NATIONAL PARK SERVICE, AND FOR OTHER PURPOSES

HEARING HELD IN WASHINGTON, DC
JUNE 10, 1994

Serial No. 103–93

Printed for the use of the Committee on Natural Resources

U.S. GOVERNMENT PRINTING OFFICE

84–710 WASHINGTON : 1994

For sale by the U.S. Government Printing Office
Superintendent of Documents, Congressional Sales Office, Washington, DC 20402
ISBN 0-16-046324-6

COMMITTEE ON NATURAL RESOURCES

GEORGE MILLER, California, *Chairman*

PHILIP R. SHARP, Indiana
EDWARD J. MARKEY, Massachusetts
AUSTIN J. MURPHY, Pennsylvania
NICK JOE RAHALL II, West Virginia
BRUCE F. VENTO, Minnesota
PAT WILLIAMS, Montana
RON DE LUGO, Virgin Islands
SAM GEJDENSON, Connecticut
RICHARD H. LEHMAN, California
BILL RICHARDSON, New Mexico
PETER A. DEFAZIO, Oregon
ENI F.H. FALEOMAVAEGA, American Samoa
TIM JOHNSON, South Dakota
LARRY LAROCCO, Idaho
NEIL ABERCROMBIE, Hawaii
CALVIN M. DOOLEY, California
CARLOS ROMERO-BARCELÓ, Puerto Rico
KARAN ENGLISH, Arizona
KAREN SHEPHERD, Utah
NATHAN DEAL, Georgia
MAURICE D. HINCHEY, New York
ROBERT A. UNDERWOOD, Guam
SAM FARR, California
LANE EVANS, Illinios
PATSY T. MINK, Hawaii
THOMAS J. BARLOW III, Kentucky
THOMAS M. BARRETT, Wisconsin

DON YOUNG, Alaska,
Ranking Republican Member
JAMES V. HANSEN, Utah
BARBARA F. VUCANOVICH, Nevada
ELTON GALLEGLY, California
ROBERT F. (BOB) SMITH, Oregon
CRAIG THOMAS, Wyoming
JOHN J. DUNCAN, JR., Tennessee
JOEL HEFLEY, Colorado
JOHN T. DOOLITTLE, California
WAYNE ALLARD, Colorado
RICHARD H. BAKER, Louisiana
KEN CALVERT, California
SCOTT MCINNIS, Colorado
RICHARD W. POMBO, California
JAY DICKEY, Arkansas

JOHN LAWRENCE, *Staff Director*
STANLEY SCOVILLE, *General Counsel*
DANIEL VAL KISH, *Republican Staff Director*

SUBCOMMITTEE ON NATIONAL PARKS, FORESTS AND PUBLIC LANDS

BRUCE F. VENTO, Minnesota, *Chairman*

EDWARD J. MARKEY, Massachusetts
NICK JOE RAHALL II, West Virginia
PAT WILLIAMS, Montana
PETER A. DEFAZIO, Oregon
TIM JOHNSON, South Dakota
LARRY LAROCCO, Idaho
NEIL ABERCROMBIE, Hawaii
CARLOS ROMERO-BARCELÓ, Puerto Rico
KARAN ENGLISH, Arizona
KAREN SHEPHERD, Utah
MAURICE D. HINCHEY, New York
ROBERT A. UNDERWOOD, Guam
AUSTIN J. MURPHY, Pennsylvania
BILL RICHARDSON, New Mexico
PATSY T. MINK, Hawaii

JAMES V. HANSEN, Utah,
Ranking Republican Member
ROBERT F. (BOB) SMITH, Oregon
CRAIG THOMAS, Wyoming
JOHN J. DUNCAN, JR., Tennessee
JOEL HEFLEY, Colorado
JOHN T. DOOLITTLE, California
RICHARD H. BAKER, Louisiana
KEN CALVERT, California
JAY DICKEY, Arkansas

RICHARD HEALY, *Staff Director*
ALEXANDER (SANDY) SCOTT, *Professional Staff Member*
CHARLENE SEAMENS, *Clerk*
STEPHEN HODAPP, *Republican Consultant on National Parks*

CONTENTS

APPENDIX

JUNE 10, 1994

H.R. 4533, TO PROMOTE ENTREPRENEURIAL MANAGEMENT OF THE NATIONAL PARK SERVICE, AND FOR OTHER PURPOSES

FRIDAY, JUNE 10, 1994.

HOUSE OF REPRESENTATIVES,
COMMITTEE ON NATURAL RESOURCES,
SUBCOMMITTEE ON NATIONAL PARKS, FORESTS
AND PUBLIC LANDS,
Washington, DC.

The subcommittee met, pursuant to call, at 9:00 a.m. in room 1324, Longworth House Office Building, Hon. Bruce F. Vento [chairman of the subcommittee] presiding.

STATEMENT OF HON. BRUCE F. VENTO

Mr. VENTO. Let's get started if we can. To bring you all here at 9:00 and then to visit for a while is pleasant, but it doesn't accomplish the reason for being here so early. We appreciate the cooperation of the Park Service and the other witnesses in rearranging their schedules so that we could respond to the demands of the House schedule.

The committee will be in order.

Today we are hearing testimony on the measure H.R. 4533, legislation I introduced at the request of the National Park Service and the administration to provide expanded authority for the collection of entrance and user fees at units of the National Park System, to establish partnerships and seek donations from the private sector.

The bill is a high priority for the National Park Service; the director, Roger Kennedy; the Assistant Secretary for Fish and Wildlife and Parks, George Frampton; both of whom are with us this morning; and of course for Secretary Babbitt himself. Some of the elements of the bill were included in Vice President Gore's National Performance Review.

I appreciate, the administration's effort to seek methods of increasing revenues to help pay for the preservation of the natural and cultural resources of the National Park System. While I do not support all elements of the bill, I believe it is important for Members to be able to review the proposal and for the administration to have the opportunity to make its case for the measure. I look forward to working with the administration and other Members in reviewing and refining this proposal.

I am impressed with the National Park Service's work on the several measures before the committee before the Memorial Day recess. Such effort and constructive engagement with the administration, the Park Service, raises new hope.

Questions remain today, however, as to whether or not a real bipartisanship can be achieved in this. Events of this past week seem to have cast a shadow over such prospect. Some parties just are not up to facing the reality of compromise based on the actions to date in spite of the efforts by the Park Service and the majority in this committee.

The fee portion in this bill would eliminate the current caps and statutory prohibitions on entrance fees and give the Secretary of the Interior wide discretion to set recreation and user fees. Candidly, entrance fee, and user fee authority exists today but is not implemented. As we recall, last year the Inspector General did a probably somewhat skewed study in terms of pointing out there is $105 million worth of fees that are not collected. I think that even if you cut that in half or a third, you probably recognize there is a serious credibility gap between the Washington administration's requests and the implementation of law on the ground. Notwithstanding that varied and extensive efforts have been made to facilitate such collection, it doesn't happen. Furthermore, the promise that revenues generated and the existing laws themselves have not ensured that such revenue is supplemental rather than supplanting funding already in place.

The good intentions of the 1995 budget submission by the administration is nearly stillborn regarding this particular aspect. Whether it can translate into something different in 1996 I don't know. This is disappointing. This aspect is disappointing. It is hardly a good way to begin, and it is hard to describe the frustration that I am experiencing over provisions of law in the late 1980s that we wrote that do this.

Finally, although the bill does not indicate what new fees may be imposed, the National Park Service does have a set of proposed fees which I hope to hear more about today or in the near future.

The bill contains three management elements as well as this entrance fee business dealing with expanding the challenge cost share program, authorizing National Park Service employees to seek donations, and authorizing the Secretary to recover restitution on account of damage to park resources or park resulting from vandalism and accidental damage. This last proposal was the subject of the House legislation, I believe in 1989, which didn't make it in the Senate.

In any case, the other aspect of this is, are these entrance fees consistent with what happens in other agencies with user fees as they all sort of plug into the Land and Water Conservation Fund? I know that this makes life more complicated. Nevertheless, it is also something that we would like to address, although I don't want to send this bill winging its way to the Agriculture Committee insofar as it is an Interior matter from a jurisdiction standpoint, which is my problem, not the problem of those at the table. I just think it is imperative that we try to provide some consistency in terms of not confusing the public as to where we are going.

As I looked over the range of issues, as an example, I found that the user fees collected by the Corps of Engineers was nearly equal to the user fees collected by some of the other land management agencies. So it just gives an insight into where the revenue flows.

Other members may have opening statements. I will put my complete statement in the record.

[Prepared statement of Mr. Vento follows:]

OPENING STATEMENT OF CONGRESSMAN BRUCE F. VENTO

The Subcommittee on National Parks, Forests and Public Lands will come to order.

Today we are hearing testimony on H.R. 4533, legislation I introduced at the request of the National Park Service to provide expanded authority for the collection of entrance and user fees at national park system units and to give greater flexibility to the National Park Service to establish partnerships and seek donations from the private sector.

This bill is a high priority of National Park Service Director Roger Kennedy, Assistant Secretary for Fish, Wildlife and Parks, George Frampton and Secretary Babbitt. Some of the elements of the bill were included in Vice President Gore's National Performance Review. I appreciate the administration's effort to seek methods of increasing revenues to help pay for the preservation of the natural and cultural resources of the National Park System. While I do not support all elements of the bill, I believe it is important for members to be able to review the proposal and for the administration to have the opportunity to make its case for the legislation. I look forward to working with the administration and other members in reviewing and refining this proposal.

The fee portion of the bill would eliminate the current caps and statutory prohibitions on entrance fees and give the Secretary of the Interior wide discretion to set entrance, recreation and special use fees. Although the bill does not indicate what new fees may be imposed, the National Park Service does have a set of proposed fees which I hope to hear more about today. The bill also contains three entrepreneurial management elements dealing with expanding the challenge cost share program, authorizing National Park Service employees to seek donations and authorizing the Secretary to recover restitution on account of damage to park resources or property resulting from vandalism or accidental damages.

[Text of H.R. 4533 and background information follow:]

I

103D CONGRESS
2D SESSION

H. R. 4533

To promote entrepreneurial management of the National Park Service, and for other purposes.

IN THE HOUSE OF REPRESENTATIVES

MAY 26, 1994

Mr. VENTO (by request) introduced the following bill; which was referred to the Committee on Natural Resources

A BILL

To promote entrepreneurial management of the National Park Service, and for other purposes.

Be it enacted by the Senate and House of Representatives of the United States of America in Congress assembled,

SECTION 1. SHORT TITLE.

This Act may be cited as the "National Park Service Entrepreneurial Management Reform Act".

SEC. 2. FINDINGS.

In furtherance of the Act of August 25, 1916 (39 Stat. 535), as amended (16 U.S.C. 1, 2–4), which directs the Secretary of the Interior to administer areas of the National Park System in accordance with the fundamental purpose of conserving the scenery, wildlife, natural and historic objects, and providing for their enjoyment in a manner that will leave them unimpaired for the enjoyment of future generations, the Congress finds that—

(1) management of the National Park System requires entrepreneurial strategies that will enable the National Park Service to meet the increasing demands placed on the System by the American public; and

(2) in order to preserve the natural and cultural resources of the System for future generations and provide for appropriate enjoyment of those resources, the National Park Service must increase revenues by reforming the nature, level and collection of fees, and increasing voluntary donations and partnerships.

SEC. 3. DEFINITIONS.

As used in this Act, the term—

(1) "park" means a unit of the National Park System; and

(2) "Secretary" means the Secretary of the Interior.

SEC. 4. FEES.

(a) ADMISSION FEES.—

(1) IN GENERAL.—The Secretary shall establish reasonable admission fees to be charged at units of

the National Park System where the Secretary determines that such fees are appropriate and feasible.

(2) ANNUAL PASSES.—For admission or entrance into any unit of the National Park System designated by the Secretary pursuant to this section, or into several specific units located in a particular geographic area, or for entrance to all units where an admission fee is charged, the Secretary is authorized to make available annual admission permits for reasonable fees to be determined by the Secretary.

(3) SINGLE VISITS.—The Secretary shall establish reasonable admission fees for a single visit at any unit of the National Park System designated by the Secretary pursuant to this section for persons who choose not to purchase an annual pass.

(b) RECREATION USE FEES.—The Secretary shall establish reasonable fees for specialized outdoor recreation sites, facilities, equipment, or services that are provided or furnished at Federal expense.

(c) SPECIAL PARK USES.—The Secretary shall establish reasonable fees for uses of park units that require special arrangements including permits. The fees shall cover all costs of providing necessary services associated with special uses and shall be credited to the appropriation current at that time.

(d) RETENTION OF FEES.—(1) Except as provided below, fees collected pursuant to subsections 4 (a) and (b) of this Act shall be deposited in the special fund account established in Section 4 of the Land and Water Conservation Fund Act of 1965 (16 U.S.C. 460 1–6a(i)(4)).

(2) Notwithstanding any other provision of law, beginning in fiscal year 1995 and thereafter, an amount equal to 15 percent of the total fees collected in the immediate preceding fiscal year pursuant to subsections 4 (a) and (b) shall be deducted from the current year collections and shall be deposited into a special fund established in the Treasury of the United States titled "Fee Collection Support—National Park System" and shall be available to the Secretary without further appropriation to cover the costs of collection of the fees, to remain available until expended.

(3) Notwithstanding any other provision of law, beginning in fiscal year 1996 and thereafter, 50 percent of the difference in additional receipts collected during the immediate preceding fiscal year as compared to total receipts collected in fiscal year 1993 shall be deducted from the current year collections and shall be covered into a special fund established in the Treasury of the United States titled "National Park Renewal Fund", and shall be available to the Secretary without further appropriation

for infrastructure needs at parks, including but not limited to facility refurbishment, repair and replacement, resource protection, interpretive/educational media (exhibits), and other infrastructure projects beneficial to park resources, to remain available until expended.

(4) In fiscal year 1995 only, fees authorized to be collected pursuant to subsections 4 (a) and (b) of this Act may be collected only to the extent provided in advance in appropriations acts and shall be credited to the appropriate special fund accounts described in this Act. In addition, said fees shall be available for the purposes of this Act only to the extent provided in advance in appropriations acts and are authorized to be appropriated to remain available until expended. In fiscal year 1996 and thereafter, fees collected as authorized to be collected pursuant to subsections 4 (a) and (b) of this Act may be collected as authorized by this Act and shall be available as provided in this Act without further provision in appropriations acts.

(e) USE OF FEES.—The Secretary shall develop procedures for the use of these receipts that ensure accountability and demonstrated results consistent with the purposes of this Act. The Secretary shall report annually to Congress on the expenditure of funds from fees collected, beginning after the first full fiscal year following enactment of this Act.

(f) DISCOUNTS.—In establishing the fees authorized in this section, the Secretary shall establish appropriate discounts for educational groups, persons sixty-two years of age older, or persons who are blind or permanently disabled. The Secretary may also establish criteria when the fees may be waived for these groups or individuals.

(g) CRITERIA.—All fees established pursuant to this section shall be fair and equitable, taking into consideration the direct and indirect cost to the Government, the benefits to the recipient, the public policy or interest served, the comparable fees charged by non-Federal public and private agencies, the economic and administrative feasibility of fee collection and other pertinent factors. The Secretary shall from time to time review the fees for consistency with the provisions of this subsection and provide timely public notice of any proposed changes in the fees.

SEC. 5. DONATIONS.

(a) REQUESTS FOR DONATIONS.—In addition to other authorities the Secretary may have to accept the donation of lands, buildings, other property, services, and moneys for the purposes of the National Park System, the Secretary is authorized to solicit donations of money, property, and services from individuals, corporations, foundations and other potential donors who the Secretary believes would wish to make such donations as an expression of support for the national parks. Such donations may be accepted and used for any authorized purpose or program of the National Park Service, and donations of money shall remain available for expenditure without fiscal year limitation. Any employees of the Department to whom this authority is delegated shall be set forth in regulations issued by the Secretary pursuant to paragraph (d).

(b) EMPLOYEE PARTICIPATION.—Employees of the National Park Service may solicit donations only if the request is incidental to or in support of, and does not interfere with their primary duty of protecting and administering the parks or administering authorized programs, and only for the purpose of providing a level of resource protection, visitor facilities, or services for health and safety projects, recurring maintenance activities, or for other routine activities normally funded through annual agency appropriations. Such requests must be in accordance with guidelines issued pursuant to paragraph (d).

(c) PROHIBITIONS.—(1) A donation may not be accepted in exchange for a commitment to the donor on the part of the National Park Service or which attaches conditions inconsistent with applicable laws and regulations or that is conditioned upon or will require the expenditure of appropriated funds that are not available to the Department, or which compromises a criminal or civil position of the United States or any of its departments or agencies or the administrative authority of any agency of the United States.

(2) In utilizing the authorities contained in this section employees of the National Park Service shall not directly conduct or execute major fund raising campaigns, but may cooperate with others whom the Secretary may designate to conduct such campaigns on behalf of the National Park Service.

(d) REGULATIONS AND GUIDANCE.—The Secretary shall issue regulations setting forth those positions to which he has delegated his authority under paragraph (a) and the categories of employees of the National Park Service that are authorized to request donations pursuant to paragraph (b). Such regulations shall also set forth any limitations on the types of donations that will be requested or accepted as well as the sources of those donations.

(2) The Secretary shall publish guidelines which set forth the criteria to be used in determining whether the solicitation or acceptance of contributions of lands, buildings, other property, services, moneys and other gifts or donations authorized by this section would reflect unfavorably upon the ability of the Department of the Interior

ably upon the ability of the Department of the Interior or any employee to carry out its responsibilities or official duties in a fair and objective manner, or would compromise the integrity or the appearance of the integrity of its programs or any official involved in those programs. The Secretary shall also issue written guidance on the extent of the cooperation that may be provided by National Park Service employees in any major fund raising campaign which the Secretary has designated others to conduct pursuant to paragraph (c)(2).

SEC. 6. CHALLENGE COST-SHARE AGREEMENTS.

(a) AGREEMENTS.—The Secretary is authorized to negotiate and enter into challenge cost-share agreements with cooperators. For purposes of this section, the term—

(1) "challenge cost-share agreement" means any agreement entered into between the Secretary and any cooperator for the purpose of sharing costs or services in carrying out authorized functions and responsibilities of the Secretary with respect to the National Park System; and

(2) "cooperator" means any State or local government, public or private agency, organization, institution, corporation, individual, or other entity.

(b) USE OF FEDERAL FUNDS.—In carrying out challenge cost-share agreements, the Secretary is authorized, subject to appropriation, to provide the Federal funding share from any funds available to the National Park Service.

SEC. 7. COST RECOVERY FOR DAMAGE TO PARK RESOURCES.

Any funds payable to United States as restitution on account of damage to park resources or property shall be paid to the Secretary. Any such funds, and any other funds received by the Secretary as a result of forfeiture, compromise, or settlement on account of damage to park resources or property shall be available without appropriation and may be expended by the Secretary without regard to fiscal year limitation to improve, protect, or rehabilitate any park resources or property which have been damaged by the action of a permittee or any unauthorized person.

SEC. 8. CONSISTENCY WITH OTHER LAWS.

(a) Except as provided in subsection (b), to the extent that the provisions of this Act are inconsistent with section 4 of the Land and Water Conservation Act of 1965 as amended (16 U.S.C. 4601–6a) or any other provision of law, including any provision that prohibits or limits the charging of a reasonable recreation or other fee, the provisions of this Act shall prevail.

84-710 O – 94 – 2

(b) The following sections of the Land and Water Conservation Act of 1965 as amended (16 U.S.C. 4601–6a) will apply to this Act:

(1) RULES AND REGULATIONS; ESTABLISHMENT; ENFORCEMENT POWERS; PENALTY FOR VIOLATIONS.—In accordance with the provisions of this section, the Secretary may prescribe rules and regulations for areas under his or her administration for the collection of any fee established pursuant to this section. Persons authorized to enforce any such rules or regulations issued under this subsection may, within areas under the administration or authority of the Secretary and with or, if the offense is committed in his presence, without a warrant, arrest any person who violates such rules and regulations. Any person so arrested may be tried and sentenced by the United States magistrate judge specifically designated for that purpose by the court by which he was appointed, in the same manner and subject to the same conditions as provided in subsections (b), (c), (d), and (e) of section 3401 of title 18. Any violations of the rules and regulations issued under this subsection shall be punishable by a fine of not more than $1,000.

(2) CRITERIA, POSTING AND UNIFORMITY OF FEES.—Clear notice that a fee has been established pursuant to this section shall be prominently posted at each area and at appropriate locations therein and shall be included in publications distributed at such areas.

(3) CONTRACTS WITH PUBLIC OR PRIVATE ENTITIES FOR VISITOR RESERVATION SERVICES.—The Secretary, under such terms and conditions as he deems appropriate, may contract with any public or private entity to provide visitor reservation services. Any such contract may provide that the contractor shall be permitted to deduct a commission to be fixed by the agency head from the amount charged the public for providing such services and to remit the net proceeds therefrom to the contracting agency.

(4) FEDERAL AND STATE LAWS UNAFFECTED.—Nothing in this Act shall authorize Federal hunting or fishing licenses or fees or charges for commercial or other activities not related to recreation, nor shall it affect any rights or authority of the States with respect to fish and wildlife, nor shall it repeal or modify any provision of law that permits States or political subdivisions to share in the reve-

nues from Federal lands or any provision of law that provides that any fees or charges collected at particular Federal areas shall be used for or credited to specific purposes or special funds as authorized by that provision of law.

(5) SELLING OF PERMITS AND COLLECTION OF FEES BY VOLUNTEERS AT DESIGNATED AREAS; COLLECTING AGENCY DUTIES; SURETY BONDS; SELLING OF ANNUAL ADMISSION PERMITS BY PUBLIC AND PRIVATE ENTITIES UNDER ARRANGEMENTS WITH COLLECTING AGENCY HEAD.—When authorized by the Secretary, volunteers at designated areas may sell permits and collect fees authorized or established pursuant to this section. The Secretary shall ensure that such volunteers have adequate training regarding—

(A) the sale of permits and the collection of fees,

(B) the purposes and resources of the areas in which they are assigned, and

(C) the provision of assistance and information to visitors to the designated area.

The Secretary shall require a surety bond for any such volunteer performing services under this subsection. Funds available to the collecting agency may be used to cover the cost of any such surety bond. The head of the collecting agency may enter into arrangements with qualified public or private entities pursuant to which such entities may well (without cost to the United States) annual admission permits (including Golden Eagle Passports) at any appropriate location.

○

BACKGROUND ON H.R. 4533, NATIONAL PARK SERVICE ENTREPRENEURIAL MANAGEMENT REFORM ACT

H.R. 4533, the National Park Service Entrepreneurial Management Reform Act, is legislation proposed by the National Park Service. A number of the elements in the bill were recommended in Vice President Al Gore's National Performance Review.

The fee portion of the bill would give the Secretary of the Interior wide discretion to set entrance, recreation and special use fees. The bill would remove the current caps on entrance fees, which limit entrance fees to $5 per vehicle or $3 per individual. Current statutory prohibitions on entrance fee collection at specific parks would also be eliminated, but the criteria of current Land and Water Conservation Fund concerning feasibility, costs of collection and benefits to visitors would still apply. Although the proposal would make it possible for entrance fees to be imposed at any unit of the National Park System, the National Park Service has indicated that they will not charge entrance fees at certain park units, to be determined at a later date. The bill also contains a new "special park use fee" which would allow NPS to charge event holders the NPS costs for staffing an event.

H.R. 4533 provides that beginning in Fiscal Year 1996, the National Park Service would keep 50% of new recreation fees collected. These monies would go into a "National Park Renewal Fund" which would be available without further appropriation for infrastructure needs at national park units. These would include facility repair and replacement, resource protection, interpretive exhibits and other projects. The Park Renewal Funds would be distributed as follows: 50% to the collecting parks and 50% to non-collecting parks. The rest of the recreation fees (the 50% not going in the Park Renewal Fund) would go into the recreation fee account and be appropriated for park purposes in the following fiscal year. Thus the main difference between current law and the new proposal is that 50% of the new recreation fees collected would not be subject to further appropriations. The bill continues the provision included in P.L. 103-66 (the Omnibus Reconciliation Act of 1993) which provides that 15% of recreation fees could be retained without further appropriation to cover the costs of collection.

The National Park Service has not provided a list of proposed entrance fees or other specific changes they would make if this legislation were enacted. However, they have indicated they are actively considering the following steps:
(1) eliminating the practice of charging entrance fees per vehicle and replacing it with a per person fee; (2) revising per person rates to $5 for prime parks and $4 for intermediate parks; (3) increasing the price of the Golden Eagle Passport to $35; and (4) instituting a half price fee for Golden Age Passport holders.

Page 2

The National Park Service did provide a breakdown of the $32 million in potential increased revenues they assumed for Fiscal Year 1995. The breakdown is as follows:

Increased Visitation	$ 2 million
Boat Launching	$ 1.5 million
Camping	$ 1.0 million
Commercial Tours	$ 4.5 million
Golden Age Passport	$ 3.0 million
User Fee Increases	$ 3.0 million
New Entrance and User Fees	$12.0 million
Private Sector Golden Eagle Sales	$ 1.0 million
Entrance Fee Increases	$ 7.0 million
TOTAL	$32 million

H.R. 4355 would make three changes to encourage entrepreneurial management at the National Park Service. First, it would authorize the Secretary of the Interior and certain National Park Service employees to seek donations of money, property and services from foundations, corporations and other potential donors, subject to certain guidelines. Although the National Park Service has received many donations, their authority to solicit donations has been ambiguous. Second, it would authorize the Secretary to recover restitution on account of damage to park resources or property resulting from vandalism or accidental damages. Settlement money would go to the National Park Service for park purposes. Third, the bill expands the current "Challenge Cost-Share" program to allow any funds appropriated for the operation of the National Park Service to be used to carry out Challenge Cost-Share agreements. This would make the NPS program operate more like the successful Challenge Cost-Share program of the Forest Service. Instead of having a small line item appropriation for Challenge Cost-Share nationwide, park managers could use general operations and maintenance funding to develop Challenge Cost-Share projects. This would encourage park managers to seek cooperators for projects such as trail maintenance.

FEE PROVISIONS OF 1993 OMNIBUS RECONCILIATION ACT

P.L. 103-66, the Omnibus Reconciliation Act of 1993, contained several significant changes in law concerning entrance and user fees at the federal land managing agencies. The provisions which applied to the National Park Service are listed below:

- It authorized user fees at day use recreation sites, including swimming areas, boat ramps and managed parking lots on NPS lands. It loosened requirements for charging for overnight camping.

• It authorized the present and future direct costs of collection to be deducted from fee revenue but capped this amount at 15% of fee revenue collected for that year.

• It imposed a one-time processing fee of $10 for Golden Age Passports.

• It authorized the sale of Golden Eagle Passports by non-federal entities. This provision has not been implemented yet.

• It authorized a commercial tour use fee for vehicles and airplanes entering National Park System units for the sole purpose of providing commercial tour services. This provision has been implemented for vehicles but not for aircraft.

HISTORY OF RECREATION FEES

The collection of fees from users of national parks and recreation areas dates back to 1908, when fees for automobiles were instituted at Mount Ranier National Park. Over the next half century, the fee collection system grew in national parks and spread to other federal land managing agencies through a series of special laws, regulations and administrative decisions.

The Land and Water Conservation Fund (LWCF) Act of 1965 (P.L. 88-578) was the first legislation to authorize a uniform fee system for outdoor recreation in all Federal recreation areas. The fee provisions of the LWCF Act were amended eight different times prior to the comprehensive fee legislation enacted in 1987 as part of the Omnibus Budget Reconciliation Act (P.L. 100-203).

Current Law

Currently, seven Federal land managing agencies (National Park Service, Fish and Wildlife Service, Bureau of Land Management, Bureau of Reclamation, Forest Service, Army Corps of Engineers, and Tennessee Valley Authority) are authorized to charge user fees at areas where specialized outdoor recreation facilities, equipment, or services are provided at public expense. Examples of user fees include camping, specialized boat launching facilities and parking fees. The National Park Service and the Fish and Wildlife Service are the only agencies which charge entrance fees, although the Forest Service recently has been authorized to charge admission fees at certain areas.

There are currently five federal recreation passes to promote the enjoyment of park and recreation areas and national wildlife refuges managed by the federal government. These are:

The Golden Eagle Pass costs $25 and is valid for one calendar year. It admits pass holders and accompanying passengers in their vehicles into all National Park units and wildlife refuges at no charge. It does not cover user charges such as camping and parking. In FY91, $3,400,000 was raised from the sale of Golden Eagle passes.

The Park Pass is an annual entrance pass to a specific park, monument or recreation area in the National Park system. In some cases, more than one nearby or related park is included. The pass costs $10 or $15 and does not cover user fees. In FY91, $1,540,864 was collected from the sale of annual park passes.

The Golden Age Passport is a free lifetime entrance permit admitting persons age 62 or older to parks, monuments, recreation areas, and national wildlife refuges. It also provides a 50% discount on Federal user fees for facilities and services such as camping and parking. The passport admits the passport holder and accompanying vehicle passengers.

The Golden Access Passport is a free lifetime entrance permit admitting blind or permanently disabled persons to any park, monument, refuge or recreation area which charges fees.

The Federal Duck Stamp is required for all waterfowl hunters over age 16 and also serves as an annual entrance fee permit to national wildlife refuges which charge entrance fees.

Entrance Fees

Currently 136 units of the National Park System charge entrance fees. The maximum entrance fee is $10 per vehicle at Grand Teton, Yellowstone and Grand Canyon National Parks and $5 or $3 per vehicle at other park units. Entrance fees for individuals are $4 at Grand Teton, Yellowstone and Grand Canyon National Parks and $2 or $1 at other parks. In FY91, $41.1 million was collected in daily entrance fees at units of the National Park System. Of the 386 National Wildlife Refuges which are open to the public, 23 charge entrance fees. In FY91, $1.5 million was collected in daily entrance fees at National Wildlife Refuges which charge entrance fees. No other federal agencies charge entrance fees. However, the Forest Service does have the authority to do so.

Page 5

User Fees and Special Permits

All seven land management agencies collect user fees for specialized outdoor recreation facilities, equipment or services provided at public expense. Special permits for uses such as group activities, recreation events and motorized recreation can be issued and fees can be charged.

The following table provides a breakdown by agency of funds collected by entrance and user fees in Fiscal Year 1991. The data is from the 1991 Federal Recreation Fee Report to Congress compiled by the Department of Interior.

Federal Agency	User Fee Receipts	Entrance Fee Receipts	Total Fee Receipts (2)
National Park Service	$18,128,280	$41,056,745	$59,185,025
Army Corps of Engineers	$18,439,674	$0	$18,439,674
Forest Service	$14,957,894	$0	$14,957,894
Fish and Wildlife Service	$331,068	$1,545,105 (1)	$1,876,173
Bureau of Land Management	$1,802,821	$0	$1,802,821
Tennessee Valley Authority	$916,200	$0	$916,200
Bureau of Reclamation	$712,219	$0	$712,219

1 Receipts from the sale of Federal Duck Stamps as entrance fees are included in this figure

2 These are the totals for each agency of all Golden Eagle Pass receipts, user fee receipts and entrance fee receipts.

Distribution of Recreation Fees

Under current law, user and entrance fees collected by any agency other than the National Park Service are to be made available for resource protection, research, interpretation and maintenance activities related to resource protection.

For the National Park Service, entrance fee receipts are to be used for resource protection, research and interpretation at units of the National Park System. User fee receipts are to be used for resource protection, research, interpretation and maintenance of activities related to resource protection. Funds are to be distributed as follows: 10% to be allocated by the Director of the National Park Service on the basis of need; 40% to be allocated to all park units based on their operation costs and 50% to be allocated to the collecting parks on the basis of how much each park unit collected. The National Park Service has not been able to demonstrate compliance with these mandates for distribution of recreation fees.

Mr. VENTO. Mr. Thomas.

STATEMENT OF HON. CRAIG THOMAS

Mr. THOMAS. Thank you, Mr. Chairman. I just have a comment or two.

I am sorry I don't quite understand your pessimism this morning or I would give you some comfort, but I don't know exactly what you are talking about.

Let me say that I think it makes some sense to move towards some fee restructuring. There is a great backlog of needs obviously. It is going to be more and more difficult to get funds. There is a great deal of talk about underpayment on the part of grazers and miners and everyone else. Perhaps there is an underpayment on the part of recreationalists as well, and perhaps that is what we ought to talk about.

I am always a little confused—have been recently. It seems everything the administration does is either reform or reinvent or revolutionize. As I read this, this is hardly reform, but that is what it is called apparently.

As you know, I have a special interest in Yellowstone and Teton, and I must tell you, I had the notion from talking with Dick Cheney a number of years ago that some of this money that is collected in the park stays in the park. Now I am told that it doesn't at all. I am disappointed in that, frankly.

It would seem to me that the parks that draw the greatest attention are the ones that probably need the greatest resources to keep the facilities there. I am certain that is true in Yellowstone; I am certain that is true in Teton. So I hope that we can do something about that.

I must tell you that I also have a concern that, to the extent that these fees would be kept in a particular park, I suspect the appropriators would be aware of that and make the adjustments in the appropriations to where you may not make a great deal of headway with respect to it.

It is also my understanding that this would raise somewhere between $30 and $35 million. That is a lot of money, but it certainly is not much of a reform in terms of the half a billion or billions of dollars that are needed to keep the place fixed up. But, nevertheless, it is a step in the right direction.

But short of reform, gentlemen, you talked about reinventing it. If this is reinventing, why, I am a little surprised, and maybe you will comment on that just a little bit. Thank you for being here. I appreciate what you do.

Mr. VENTO. Congressman Calvert.

Mr. CALVERT. I will just submit my opening statement for the record. Thank you.

Mr. VENTO. Thanks for being here.

[Prepared statement of Mr. Calvert follows:]

Committee on Natural Resources

Subcommittee on National Parks, Forests, and Public Lands

June 10, 1994

Remarks by Ken Calvert

Thank you, Mr. Chairman:

I look forward to today's hearing on the National Park Service Entrepreneurial Management Reform Act.

During the 103rd Congress we have heard testimony before this subcommittee on the National Parks Service's inability to refurbish dilapidated parks like the Yosemite and Grand Canyon because they are experiencing a budget shortfall of over $400 million. To relieve the agency's budget problem, we have heard several suggestions...concession reform, employee cutbacks and now, higher recreation fees. To be honest, I have questions as to how much a cost-saver H.R. 4533 will be.

The constituents in my district of Riverside, California have enjoyed the multi-use and recreation opportunities in Cleveland National Forest and the desert for many years. They want to continue to enjoy these natural resources and therefore do not mind paying a nominal recreation fee. However, I object to having my constituents pay a higher user fee if the money does not go back into the agency's park maintenance program. I suspect that any money raised through additional user and consession fees will go toward the proposed $300 million dollar land acquisition in the California desert or the Presidio in the bay area.

I am anxious to see this subcommittee reach a fair and rational solution to a problem that continues to plague the National Park Service. In a time of deficit reduction and tight budget cuts I hope that this subcommittee will have better insight into solving the agency's budget shortfall and future problems.

Thank you, Mr. Chairman.

Mr. VENTO. We are pleased to welcome Director Kennedy and the Assistant Secretary, Mr. Frampton.

Which one of you is going to go first here?

Assistant Secretary Frampton, we have a statement—Mr. Kennedy's statement. Mr. Frampton, would you please proceed with your informal statement.

PANEL CONSISTING OF GEORGE FRAMPTON, ASSISTANT SECRETARY, WILDLIFE AND PARKS, U.S. DEPARTMENT OF THE INTERIOR; AND ROGER G. KENNEDY, DIRECTOR, NATIONAL PARK SERVICE, U.S. DEPARTMENT OF THE INTERIOR, ACCOMPANIED BY MICHAEL FINLEY, ACTING ASSOCIATE DIRECTOR, NATIONAL PARK SERVICE

STATEMENT OF GEORGE FRAMPTON

Mr. FRAMPTON. Thank you, Mr. Chairman.

I do not have a written statement. I am simply here and appreciate being given the opportunity on behalf of the Secretary, who is out of town today, to emphasize that dealing with the issues that are the subject of this hearing this morning, particularly fees, but also seeking ways to get more private support for the park system, are very high priorities not only for the Park Service but for the department and the Secretary personally.

Trying to find a way to develop a rational, equitable fee system that provides the right kind of incentives for superintendents to collect the fees and makes it certain that some of the money at least will go back into the park system and into that park are very high priorities, and I think there is a great deal of public support for that.

This is one of the four or five issues that the Secretary has focused on personally, in addition to concessions reform, which you have been very, very helpful and supportive on. Upgrading the pay and professionalization of the people who work in the park system and dealing with issues, ecosystem issues, like park transportation, these are the things that are the Secretary's personal highest priorities for the National Park Service, and it is clear, looking at the budget allocations and the kinds of numbers that we are looking at for 1996, fiscal year 1996, for the Park Service that, given the additional costs and the additional responsibilities as well as the backlog with which this agency is faced, that we desperately need to find better ways of building a firmer financial and economic support base under our National Parks, and this is one of the ways we can do that.

So we look forward to working with the committee, and we want to see whether we can move this bill, and we are very eager to work with you and with other Members of the House to see their concerns, if we can resolve those and if we can shape something here that is really good for the future of the National Parks.

Thank you, Mr. Chairman.

Mr. VENTO. Well, we appreciate your statement and your presence and interest. Your presence underlines the importance of this, and, as I said, I was encouraged last week and before that in terms of the concession and the heritage bill and the park study bill. We have really made a lot of progress. In any case, we hopefully will be able to overcome the remaining misunderstandings.

We are pleased to welcome Director Kennedy. Without objection the statements of all the witnesses in their entirety will be made part of the record, and hearing no objection. That would include that of the director.

Director Kennedy.

STATEMENT OF ROGER G. KENNEDY

Mr. KENNEDY. Thank you, Mr. Chairman.

Mr. Thomas's comments lead me to suggest that we adopt his language, and if we could do it unanimously we would be extremely grateful. If we could describe this as a step in the right direction, we would drop aside all hyperbolic descriptions aside from that.

Having said so, Mr. Chairman, it is clear that there is a long history of endeavor on the part of this committee and others that go to another of Mr. Thomas's points. The reason that Stephen Mather saw, too, that there were fees collected to begin with was that he could get some people to collect fees to serve the parks and thereby was able to replace with the current civilians you see before you the caliber of people who were there. Beginning in 1908, this process has been carried forward.

This is hardly a revolutionary step. Here we are in 1994 still trying to get a fee bill that provides what you have been trying to do in other contexts, which is an evenhanded and systematic address to the process of getting a little more money to do what we all need to do in the parks and to do that in a way which provides the resumption as you, both the majority and minority, have said in other contexts, to prevent a resumption of another kind of cavalry raids which happen to come from Capitol Hill in which what happens is that individual Members have a deep temptation, in the absence of a systematic approach, to fix fees here, there, differentially, and with no system, which produces not only within the Park System the kinds of disparities to which you have alluded but also with respect to the differences between the Park System, the Forest Service, the Bureau, or anyone else who is collecting fees.

It is only when you get a system established with somebody responsible to state it, with the correlations among parks stated and that person—in this case the Secretary of the Interior presumably delegated to the director of the Park Service—and that person commissioned to set up a system which you can observe, approve, disapprove, observe the effects of as it is implemented on the ground, and it is only by doing that that you can systematically relate that to what everybody else does.

Absent, we will have the current hodgepodge system which bears—where there is no system, some parks collect, some don't collect, some could that don't.

Let me address if I may, though—far more expert in this matter will be my colleague Mike Finley, who is our acting director of operation—assistant director for operations, who has actually run a park, and I'll take a whack, if I may, at why it is that we observe currently, the absence of collection of fees, even acknowledging that those fees, as it currently is, don't go to the parks.

If you were a practicing superintendent and you had to choose between the safety of your visitors or the repairs necessary to keep something in place that you need to have in place, or having somebody talk to the kids around the campfire and having someone at a way station on the way into a park to collect a fee that goes to the general revenues, what choice would you make? Under those circumstances, there is no incentive on anybody's part to reallocate their priorities.

But beyond that, beyond that, if it is true that we all—and I think it is true that everyone from Stephen Mather through Harold Ickes to this committee in great eloquence in past testimony, perhaps the most effective discussion of this subject establishing the principles upon which we all agree was in 1972 in which everybody agreed that this was a desirable—that the desirable outcome was a systematic approach to the collection of fees reviewed regularly by the Congress to be sure that it was properly implemented.

It is just worth recalling, I think, that perhaps Harold Ickes, with the kind of pungency which is characteristic of him, said that those who actually visit the parks should make contributions to their upkeep for the services they receive which are not received by other citizens.

It is also true that in the congressional debates in 1972 they said it for all of us, perhaps even for all time, it is so abundantly clear as to be almost axiomatic, the users of Federal recreation areas should contribute more to Federal recreation programs than nonusers. Not all. Goodness knows, we are not talking about all, we are talking about at best $30 or $40 million out of $1.7 billion, but certainly some more, and that seems to me to be the core of our discussion. It is how much more and how do you make certain that they are fairly collected?

The best way, it seems to us, is for us to be commissioned by you to provide you with a system that we discuss with you before it is implemented, but, much more importantly, that you can check on as it is actually implemented.

Now, finally, assenting with glee to the description of a step in the right direction, we would like to suggest that this does, indeed, as everyone in this room knows, become not a one-step but a two-step process. Once we have authorized a process that is fair and provides for accountability back to the Congress as to its implementation, then of course we have to go about the process of seeking to make sure that the desirability to the general revenues of the United States of there being additional revenues derived from users, that that desirability is recognized by the appropriations side of this body.

It is not sufficient merely that the revenue come in, it is, as all Members have suggested in past debates and have once again today made clear, essential that if that is to occur, that it cannot be offset directly by a reduction on the other side.

Now it does seem to us that if we can make it as clear as we can that park superintendents and other Park Service officials will exert themselves—and that, Mr. Thomas, it seems to me to be the chief justification to talk about entrepreneurship; it means getting out and doing it, working at it, let's get on with this—that the Park Service people will have a strong incentive to take care of the

84-710 O - 94 - 3

things they know most closely—that is, their own parks—but also in the ethic of the Park Service to serve other parks as well. If they have an incentive to do that, they will do that, and if they do do that under these provisions in this bill, some of the benefits flow to the general revenues.

In economics, the objective here is to see to it that you get more in the aggregate than it is going to cost you. That is an argument not so much perhaps for this committee, but it is an argument which seems to me to be true, desirable, and a part of the steps in the right direction.

Thank you, Mr. Chairman.

[Prepared statement of Mr. Kennedy follows:]

STATEMENT OF ROGER G.KENNEDY, DIRECTOR, NATIONAL PARK SERVICE, DEPARTMENT OF THE INTERIOR, BEFORE THE SUBCOMMITTEE ON NATIONAL PARKS, FORESTS, AND PUBLIC LANDS, HOUSE COMMITTEE ON NATURAL RESOURCES, ON H.R. 4533, THE NATIONAL PARK SERVICE ENTREPRENEURIAL MANAGEMENT REFORM ACT.

June 10, 1994

Mr. Chairman, I am pleased to appear before the Subcommittee today in strong support of H.R. 4533, the National Park Service Entrepreneurial Management Reform Act. We look forward to working with you and your staff on any technical modifications or needs to clarify authorities that this legislation would provide to the Secretary with the hope that H.R. 4533 can be enacted expeditiously.

Mr. Chairman, as you are fully aware, in the face of urgent internal needs and growing demands on park resources, the National Park Service will have difficulty in accomplishing its mission without increasing revenues. Since the present deficit reduction effort makes continued expanding appropriations unlikely to meet increasing demands placed on the system, the National Park Service must explore new means of enhancing revenues on its own. By embracing more of an entrepreneurial management strategy, this legislation will help to encourage the managers of our National Parks to find means to reinvest park visitor fees back to the parks themselves; to encourage donations to parks; to increase voluntary partnerships with the private sector; and to recover costs of repair of damages to park resources by sending restitution directly back to the parks that received the damage.

Many of the features of this legislation are recommended in the administration's National Performance Review. This legislation would provide more authority for managers at the field level to meet the needs of increasing visitation and protection of park resources. We consistently hear from park visitors that they are willing to pay reasonable fees to enjoy the quality experience available within the national parks. This bill matches these American's interest in caring for their parks with assurances that new revenues collected from park visitors will be put to work back in the parks.

The vital physical needs of National Parks must be met to leave them unimpaired for the enjoyment of future generations. Our current estimates indicate a present backlog of physical needs totalling over $5 billion. But parks and the public's expectations of parks are not static. Beyond these current needs, lie the emerging demands of the future, which require us to respond to old problems with new vision. The long-term viability of the parks do not just depend upon repairing existing infrastructure such as roads, but designing and promoting alternative transportation systems; not just improving visitor facilities but redesigning them to meet the needs of the next century; not just improving visitor services but revitalizing them with information-age technology. These reforms, and many others must integrate the natural and cultural resources of the parks within a single management strategy. This strategy will require fiscal support not available through the present appropriations process. This legislation has four primary elements that would help the National Park Service meet these present and future needs.

First, the legislation would authorize the Secretary of the Interior to set admission, recreational, and special use fees at reasonable rates. This would be accomplished by lifting current caps and eliminating some exclusions to entrance fees, by using developed criteria taking into consideration public interest and comparability in value to other facilities, as well as administrative feasibility in collecting fees. The National Park Service would be allowed to continue to use fee revenue to pay the cost of collection. Also, 50 percent of any additional receipts over the amount collected in 1993 would be authorized for infrastructure repairs and other cultural or natural resource projects in the parks. The other fifty percent of additional receipts would be available subject to appropriations, for allocation to all units of the National Park system in accordance with Section 4 of the Land and Water Conservation Fund Act of 1965.

Passage of this legislation is expected to provide increasing revenues beginning in FY95. These revenues would not be used to fund park operations, but rather for the refurbishment, repair and replacement of infrastructure within the parks. The fees received above the FY93 level would be available for use by parks without further appropriation by Congress. In FY 1996, this would mean an additional $36 million for the National Park Service.

The current state of the law gives NPS managers little reason to allocate staff to collect fees since much of the revenue collected returns directly to the federal treasury. This legislation will encourage managers to actively seek fee receipts, donations and cost share endeavors to begin to address the needs the parks.

Mr. Chairman, this legislation would allow the National Park Service to manage the entrance fee program similarly to the method we presently use to manage other fee programs. By eliminating the present caps on entrance fees in the

Land and Water Conservation Fund Act, the National Park Service would be allowed to manage the entrance fee program as it has the daily recreation use fee program since the early 1980s. In this program annual reviews are conducted to determine whether the park's current fee schedule is comparable to similar facilities in the park's service area. In addition to comparing facilities and services between NPS, other government and private facilities, other factors such as the economic status of the geographic service area influence the determination of fees. These fees are generally adjusted every three or four years. In contrast, the present entrance fee program is adjusted in amendments to the Land and Water Conservation Fund Act, generally on a piecemeal basis over a much longer time period. This can result in more dramatic changes in fees that are not necessarily based on a comprehensive review of economic factors or consideration of comparable areas within the National Park System. The result is a system that lacks consistency as demonstrated by the much higher entrance fees charged at Grand Canyon and Yellowstone compared to Yosemite, Everglades or Rocky Mountain even though most would agree that they have similar national appeal and visitor experiences.

A fee system as proposed in this legislation would also help bring consistency to not only how much is charged at units of the National Park System but also to areas that are exempt from charging fees. In 1987 an entrance fee program was initiated at Canaveral National Seashore with support from many of the local residents. In ten months nearly $400,000 was collected and park managers also noticed a dramatic decrease in the rate of crime in the park. This program was short lived however, and despite the fact that most National

Seashores across the nation charge entrance fees, this park was exempted, revenues were lost and the rate of crime again increased within the park unit. A nation-wide fee system managed by the National Park Service based upon tangible criteria would not only raise additional revenues but provide consistency and equity in the fee system.

Second, the National Park Service's existing "Challenge Cost-Share" program with partners such as local governments, private business and universities is expanded and codified. In 1993, donors matched $2 million of federal money with their own money to accomplish needed projects. This legislation would authorize the Federal funding share from any appropriated, fee or donated source to be used as matches with our partner's contributions. The purpose is to increase the money made available for these projects.

Third, the Secretary would be authorized to encourage donations of money, property and services from foundations, corporations and other potential donors as an expression of support for national parks. Certain employees of the Department of Interior could be designated to seek donations under carefully crafted regulations specifying the category of employees that may request donations, and defining limitations on the types of donations requested and the sources of those donations. The Secretary must also publish guidelines setting forth the criteria for determining when the solicitation of donations could reflect unfavorably on the Department or its employees.

Finally, the legislation authorizes restitution in cases such as vandalism or accidental damage to park resources or facilities. Repair of signs, fences and many park facilities are major expenses at many parks. Restitution would go directly to the Park Service for repair of the damage rather than to the general federal treasury.

Mr. Chairman, we acknowledge there may be ways to strengthen and improve this legislation. For example, commercial filming is now being conducted in National Park units under a special use permit and fees are presently charged for cost recovery only. If fees were charged on a value basis instead of only cost recovery, considerable benefits could be realized. Most filming companies expect to pay a use fee and are surprised to discover that present cost recovery fees in National Parks are extremely low. A change in the law would not only raise additional revenues for park purposes but also allow private landowners a better opportunity to compete for business with film makers and perhaps minimize the increasing pressure to use national parks for commercial film making.

We are committed to working with you and your staff in refining this proposal to insure that a new management system works to provide better services and facilities to the park visitor as well as preserving the natural and cultural resources of our nation's National Park System.

This concludes my prepared remarks on H.R. 4533, Mr. Chairman. I would be pleased to respond to your questions.

Mr. VENTO. Thank you, Director Kennedy, and we appreciate your statement.

One of the problems is that for a long time I think we accepted—of course, understood by each of you sitting at the table—I am told that Mr. Finley understands it—each administration has come in here in each year, and even last year your administration, with a proposal to modify and increase entrance fees each, every year almost for the last 10 years. So it obviously gets a little redundant in terms of how mesmerized the administration seemed to be with this small amount of revenue that might come from entrance and user fees.

So I hardly thought it was an area that I wanted to spend my entire creative energies on, although I did make considerable effort in 1987 and since then have done less with, of course, Congressman Thomas's predecessor, Dick Cheney, who was very helpful in that, and we made a pretty good cut at it, and I think that maybe what we would like to do is probably build on what we have done there and perhaps adjust it accordingly.

One of the major concerns—and we all ought to understand this before we get too far down the road— is that there is this sort of popular sentiment in the Park Service among most superintendents—and I know that I have heard even a superintendent sitting at the table talk to this—and that is that there ought to be a payment in terms of use of this. After all, if you go to Disney World or you go to something else, you go to the movies, you pay so much money.

Although this makes fine sense, the thing is, we provide the authority and then the superintendents have this authority and it doesn't get used. So there is a problem. You see, there is a dilemma here because I think that what happens with superintendents is that anything that they see infringing upon or discouraging people from coming through that gate, they are very likely not to want to do, because your business is based on people coming through the gate and on those numbers and so forth.

It is not a bad sentiment. I understand their dilemma. If I were in their place, I probably would act the same. So you have to recognize that particular problem, and there are a number of rationalizations that will occur which will explain why they do that. That is to say that my resources in terms of collecting it are more expensive than what I will take in. I have multiple entry points. This is an urban park, of course, and some of us—picking up on some of this, and what it does as a result in this hodgepodge of policy that you refer to.

Yes, I would be happy if you wanted me to yield, Mr. Finley.

Mr. FINLEY. Thank you, Mr. Chairman.

I think at the basis of your concerns and park management concerns are basic principles of equitability and fairness, and what we are proposing is a system that would outline increased collection of fees in those areas that are exempted, still relying on park managers to make the appropriate determinations, for example, in urban areas, is it administratively feasible to collect fees, and is it fair, is it equitable? Those things are always considerations that park managers feel strongly about.

But more importantly, I think what we would be less than candid to share with you is that we have never really had a system that allowed park managers to manage in an entrepreneurial way. We were always shifting resources from collecting at the gates to handle cardiacs, car accidents, poachers, law enforcement, and so forth.

The provisions that you gave us in the Budget Reconciliation Act allowed for the deduction of the 15 percent for fee collection personnel. Now that is very helpful and we promised to increase revenue to you by being able to deduct from the money that we should submit, money to pay fee collection personnel, but, lo and behold, again we are faced with a conundrum, and that is now we have FTE limitations where now it is not money so much that is preventing us from having fee collectors at the gates, but now we are having to allocate the FTE to the cardiacs, to the poachers, and to the other concerns, so that the same issues of responsibility and concern for the resource and concern for the visitors are now being balanced in a different way.

I think this bill gives us the opportunity, if we had some additional tools, to remedy the FTE dilemma, to address these their fairly, to meet the needs of the American public to provide the access for the specialized groups and criteria, and allow you to monitor our progress.

Mr. VENTO. Well, I appreciate that, Mr. Finley.

The concern—the base here was just a pragmatic realization that there is at the base not a bad instinct, I might add, in terms of wanting people to use the park. But I think that that is a concern. I think that what is going to happen here is, we are going to end up talking about some specific areas, we are going to talk about some destination parks that are not included.

I know there are some problems. I had received word some time back from Bill Nelson who was responsible for exempting Cape Canaveral. So I would like to look at the candidates. I don't know that it is in the cards for us. We can raise the limits in terms of what the amounts are and give you some discretion. I don't know if we want to completely leave it—relax it until we have more of a comfort level as to how this is going to be implemented.

As an example, as you just said, we provided the 15 percent modification last year for deduction from entrance and other fees as an expense. That is being able to take off the top and still has dilemmas.

I was out talking to some folks at Mount St. Helens out in Washington, and the Forest Service personnel there were explaining to me how that wasn't enough, they didn't know where that figure came up, and they couldn't really do it for 15 percent, and Mount St. Helens, if you know anything about it, there is one road in, and there are hundreds of thousands of people who visit. So I was a little perplexed as to what their problem was, and finally I just turned to the ranger and I said, "Just do it."

So I thought they were never going to get there. They have got three or four visitor centers that are magnificent. That is a wonderful resource in terms of attracting people.

I think the committee is going to have to look at destination parks, probably look at the urban areas which are not—I think we are just going to have to work on what we have just in terms of turning over all the authority.

We might be able to provide some flexibility in terms of the amounts that you want to raise. You, after all, have that flexibility now even though there are a dozen parks where you can charge a fee and you don't. That is why we are talking about that so-called $105 million figure, which I concede is not a fair assessment.

One of the other issues, and it relates to what Congressman Thomas has said, and I just want to point it out as an opening comment. I don't know if I will have time for all the specific questions today. I think it is more important to sort of advance the issue in terms of where we have to go rather than ask these specific questions. That is the issue of the appropriations process and holding the dollars within the park.

What we do today under the Land and Water Conservation Fund language is, we treat—and it is sort of a problem here, I know it has been for me. That is, we treat entrance fees in a certain way and user fees in a certain way, and then there is this sort of permit process in terms of revenue that comes in, which we had talked about previously and has been something that hadn't always been dealt with in the same context as the entrance fee and the user fee.

What we have said is that a certain amount of those dollars, 50 percent, had to stay in the park where it was collected. In fact, I think with the user fees, it is the entire user fee stays in the park where it is collected. In other words, the association is of services being provided there.

Furthermore, in order to make certain that the money was supplemental and not supplanting it, we had sort of categorized three or four areas, three areas in the case of entrance fees for research, for interpretation, and for resource protection. The purpose of that is to be certain that the money, in essence, is supplemental, that it doesn't supplant the existing regular budgets of those areas, that it would, in fact, deal with visitor services. We know we are never going to really fund the parks with that. So that is the purpose of that.

Now if somebody has some different ideas—that is sort of an insurance that that would happen. That is at least what we thought.

And then for the user fee, you have those three categories, research, interpretation, and resource protection, plus you have the maintenance of resource. Of course, none of these are enough in and of themselves to do what has to be done, and so I think—I think Mr. Finley perhaps or Mr. Frampton may know. Maybe you do, Director Kennedy. Is there any reason that we want to really not keep that particular framework? Why can't we work off the LWCF framework in terms of—that is not the issue of which parks, I guess, that is another matter, but the issue of why can't we work off the LWCF framework in terms of this to help ensure that.

If we do the 1996 date, that seems to take us out of the problem we get in trying to advance the funds for 1995 which has always been a problem, but if we pass it this year and implement that, why can't we use that LWCF framework, Mr. Finley?

Do you understand what I am asking?

Mr. FINLEY. I guess I really don't, Mr. Chairman.

Mr. KENNEDY. We are going to work at this for a second.

Mr. VENTO. Well, okay.

Mr. KENNEDY. I am instructed, Mr. Chairman, that the LWCF applies to all land management agencies and not just the Park Service.

Mr. VENTO. Of course it does, but I am talking about how the money is retained.

Mr. KENNEDY. That doesn't help your question.

Mr. VENTO. The fundamental law that we wrote in 1987—maybe I am a little bit too into depth here—is that the money is retained 50 percent by the parks and then 50 percent goes nationally, of which 10 percent—well, 40 percent goes to the other parks, and 10 percent is retained.

I am just asking why, from a user point or an entrance fee standpoint, we could not use that particular framework to accomplish what you are doing. If you want to keep 50 percent locally——

Mr. KENNEDY. Right. We think we are getting close to the response.

Mr. VENTO. You have a different construct. Your formula is even more complicated than that. If you think this is bad, you ought to look at yours. Yours is 50/50, and then it is 50 of 50, and then 50 of the other 50. Actually, I understand it.

Mr. KENNEDY. Mr. Finley thinks he does, Mr. Chairman.

Mr. VENTO. Okay.

Mr. Finley.

Mr. FINLEY. The primary difference between the existing law and this proposed bill is that the 50 percent or the amount over the 1993 base would be retained and would not be subject to appropriation, it would be retained for redistribution back to the system for identified categories—infrastructure repair, facility repair, and so forth.

Mr. VENTO. Well, I support that. I support 100 percent. In fact, I might like to push it up a little bit and see if we can get OMB and Mr. Sabo and CBO to go along with it.

But the point is, why can't we use the LWCF framework, because you depart from that framework. Why can't we use that?

Mr. KENNEDY. Mr. Chairman, we can, and what I hear from behind me so far suggests that we should. Therefore, if we could submit to you within a couple of hours any amendment to that, that sounds like sensible terms to me.

Mr. VENTO. No, but I mean the concern is that it seems to us, at least when we worked this out, we were able to convince one another that—articulating how it would be used.

There isn't enough money to do any of these things in terms of interpretation and research or resource protection, and in the case of user fees the maintenance of the resources which permits some of the money to be used for maintenance—you see, your point is that you want to use it for a lot of other things.

Mr. KENNEDY. We don't want to use it for all operations. We do want to use it for the kinds of categories which you just described.

Mr. VENTO. Yes, but you also have in your proposal infrastructure needs. My goodness.

Mr. KENNEDY. Yes, and if it would make it more crisp and restricted in its language and therefore more acceptable, the language that you suggested, subject to rapid amendment of this testimony, is highly satisfactory to us. We want to get on to getting 50 percent of this money into the parks, and whatever more we can get from the LWCF formula we would be delighted to have.

Mr. VENTO. Well, let me yield to my colleagues who have been very patient.

Mr. Thomas.

Mr. THOMAS. Thank you. I will be quick. I need to go to the BIA hearing.

As I recall, this did come from the reinventing initiative which estimated making $900 million in six years which is a hundred and some more million a year. Now we are down to 30. What happened to the original proposal?

Mr. KENNEDY. Mr. Thomas, I don't know about $900 million. If you collected as much as we think you might, you might get up to a hundred, but that is not—the range of increases that have been suggested as the first cut at what we think we can do sensibly early would only bring in around 30. It is a restricted bite. You could get more.

Mr. THOMAS. I see. You didn't know about it. It is in the chapter called "Promote Entrepreneurial Management of the National Park Service," and the last paragraph says that the recommendation should generate $900 million in six years.

Mr. FINLEY. Mr. Thomas, if I could respond to that, I think one thing that happened to that is, it ran into PAYGO and we found that some of that money would not in any event be counted as new money, regardless of whether it all came back, without being subject to appropriation, so that the benefits that were hoped to be realized, OMB said that they would not be able to count that as new money.

Mr. THOMAS. I understand. I understand that. I just get a little leery of great promotions that come out often of Interior, Mr. Secretary, and when it comes down to it they are something less than that.

I don't quite understand, I guess, and I understand the collection problem. But you say if—if you want them to collect it, why don't they collect it? They work for you, don't they?

Mr. KENNEDY. Yes, but they have to make some tough choices.

Mr. THOMAS. I understand. So do we. But if you want them to collect money and you say we want collections, why aren't there collections?

Mr. KENNEDY. Because if you or I were a working superintendent and you had to decide among too few people to do all the jobs before you, I could, of course, issue a directive, and then I would be telling the superintendent, "Don't you do those other things that you think you had better do."

Mr. THOMAS. I understand, but you can do that if you want to do it.

Mr. KENNEDY. You could do it, but if you did it, you would know, if you had any responsibility at all, that somebody might die that day because you did.

Mr. THOMAS. Oh, now wait a minute. How many people are there in Yellowstone Park working?

Mr. KENNEDY. Well, let's take somebody who has just been managing Yosemite.

84-710 O - 94 - 4

Mr. THOMAS. How many employees are there in Yellowstone Park?

Mr. FINLEY. I don't know. I manage Yosemite currently, but I can tell you how many are there.

Mr. THOMAS. Tell me.

Mr. KENNEDY. All right. There are 350 permanents and about 300 seasonals.

Mr. THOMAS. So out of 600 people, they are all saving lives?

Mr. KENNEDY. I didn't make that statement, Mr. Thomas, I merely——

Mr. THOMAS. Listen. I grew up near Yellowstone Park. I know a little about it. So that is, again, an overstatement to say that you have to take them away from saving lives to man the gate. Now that just isn't so. I don't know the answer, Mr. Director, but we need to deal with realism here.

Mr. KENNEDY. That is what I am trying to do too, Mr. Thomas, and I wouldn't make the argument to you that the necessary consequence of that decision on any particular day would be adverse to human life. I would suggest to you, though, that that is the kind of choice that people have to make.

Mr. THOMAS. Absolutely, and I have dealt with Bob Barbie on this, and you do have to make choices, but to come in and say it is either the gate or people die is not quite accurate, is it?

Mr. KENNEDY. No, sir, I didn't make that statement.

Mr. THOMAS. Yes, you did.

Mr. KENNEDY. I said that might occur—might occur.

On the other hand, if you didn't like that statement and you thought it was excessive, I certainly don't want to leave it in the record in a way that would cause you to think that the aggregate purpose here was not being——

Mr. THOMAS. I just think we ought to work it in a realistic way, and that is not realistic, and I want to work with you, and I want to work with the best way to do it. I think it ought to be done, but we come up here and we make all these statements, and then you go back, and then next year you come back and say, "Gosh, we're not doing it because the park superintendent doesn't want to do it," and so on. We need to really decide you want to do it, and I would like to work with you to do that.

But as I recall—as I said, I recall the conversations with Dick Cheney in 1987. This was going to be the case then. Right?

Mr. KENNEDY. Yes, I think—and I am happy to adjust my previous testimony if that provides in any way a suggestion that I think that there is a necessary consequence of these choices. It is just the choices currently do have to get made, and they do have to get made not just between the one purpose and another, not to color the purposes, but also within the FTE problem to which Mr. Finley alluded. And it is a real tough one. It isn't just money, it is people.

Mr. THOMAS. I guess what struck me is you say that the superintendent has to have an incentive to do it. If it is good for the Park Service, isn't that an incentive?

Mr. KENNEDY. It is a strong incentive, and as we would say back and forth to each other, I think there are other incentives as well——

Mr. THOMAS. Of course.

Mr. KENNEDY [continuing]. Against which the manager has got to make a choice. That is all.

Mr. THOMAS. I see them collect them in Teton. Don't they?

Mr. KENNEDY. I can't speak for the superintendent, but he is always allocating his troops for that purpose.

Mr. THOMAS. I would just like to work with it. But you guys need to be realistic as well. I mean you are here wanting the Congress to do something. You need to do something.

Mr. KENNEDY. Sure.

Mr. THOMAS. And you can do something.

Mr. KENNEDY. Sure.

Mr. THOMAS. And we ought to give you the authority and then next year you ought to come back and say we have done something.

Mr. KENNEDY. Amen.

Mr. THOMAS. I am going to look hard at it.

Mr. VENTO. Just to say I don't want to—I think my colleague put it pretty candidly. I don't think where there is authority to collect these and it doesn't occur that there isn't dollars. There is an explanation for it. I think it has to be, and the superintendents have to have the authority and the leeway to make determinations.

That is really, I think, the decentralized process. That is one of the real strengths of the Park Service in these instances.

So, the purpose of the parks isn't to collect a fee. That is incidental. And it is important. But they have to have the right to make decisions in this process.

In some areas it gets to be very difficult. The Tetons, I don't know what, but there are so many multiple entries explains it. To man or to put someone there all the time would be very difficult, as the gentleman well knows.

So, I don't think there is a lot of disagreement about this, but I do think that there is and has been. Being able to deduct the 15 percent should be a big factor in terms of being able to justify maintenance or more of an extensive effort, because it isn't at odds with the overall budget that that individual would have.

And, of course, all of this 15 percent is sort of an admission. They aren't going to be able to keep the money there. That is why that is going to work. If they were able to retain the dollars and adjust accordingly, there still would be a plan, diminishing returns, to have somebody out there. Then we can go to an honor system or something else at that particular point.

Congresswoman Patsy Mink is here and may have a question.

Mrs. MINK. Thank you very much, Mr. Chairman. This whole subject matter of fees is something about which my constituents have very intense feelings, and one of the reasons they are always reluctant to even consider thoughts of extending the National Park System further in Hawaii is because of the imposition of fees.

I understand that there is need to have allocated revenue resources to the National Park System to maintain the services that you now have for the public. But I don't think I share with any enthusiasm the idea of granting to the Park Service the authority to set fees on whatever basis you might determine or whatever criteria.

Along the line of the inquiry, what is the amount of fees that are now not being collected because the staff is allocated to other duties at parks where these fees ought to be collected? What is the amount of annual loss due to noncollection of fees that have already been allowed by legislation?

Mr. FINLEY. Right. We don't have an accurate estimate for that. I am not even sure that we could give you an accurate guess.

In certain instances we might, where we knew that we took people off the——

Mrs. MINK. Well, I think I have seen in reports and other things an indication of the number of persons that have visited various parks, figures showing ones that are heavily used and parts of it that are not. It would seem to me that a fairly accurate estimate could be obtained by just the visitor count that you are using in determining the use of these park facilities.

Mr. FINLEY. Prospectively, that is correct. I mean, if we were to talk about an area that currently does not charge a fee, and we looked at the visitor count, and we knew the types of individuals that visited that park, for example, whether they were foreign nationals and subject to fees or they were educational groups or under 16, like in Hawaii, and they would not be charged a fee for educational visits, and so forth, we could give you that picture.

I thought maybe the intent of your questions was those parks, let's say like Hawaii Volcanoes or so forth, that you might have a fee and that you currently don't have the staff available to collect that money, how much are you missing? And that is the information we don't have for you.

Mrs. MINK. That is the intent of my question. What are you not now collecting that ought to be collected? What is the revenue lost?

Mr. VENTO. If the gentlewoman would yield? Last year the GAO did some work on this and they suggested it was, in terms of entrance, user, and a whole plethora of fees or other types of permits, it was $105 million. But I think that is an overstatement of the amount. But even if you cut it to a third of that, you would recognize it as being a significant amount of dollars.

Mrs. MINK. And the new legislation that you are proposing, as I read it, you are expecting to increase your collections by about 36 million; is that correct?

Mr. KENNEDY. Yes, ma'am.

Mrs. MINK. Well, my suggestion is that you go after the hundred million before you take any more dollars out of my visitors.

Thank you, Mr. Chairman.

Mr. VENTO. Well, they may be taking—in maybe the same instance, I think that they are looking for flexibility that would permit them to rationalize what they do.

Mr. Smith, you had some questions, obviously, of the panel.

Mr. SMITH. Thank you, Mr. Chairman.

I just returned from Oregon Caves last week, and I want to tell you what a great job your people are doing there. It is a very small unit, as you well know. I think there are only six or seven park people there, but they do a great job.

And I think there are something like 100,000 people go through the Oregon Caves every year, down from 200,000 people.

The hypocrisy of all of this discussion to me, Mr. Director, is simply that we here in the Congress continually direct you, the Parks Department, the National Parks, to include increasing numbers of acres of land be it heritage programs, be it additions, buffer zones, and I think last year the Administration and your organization supported something like $100 million in additional acquisitions.

Recognizing at this point that your backlog in construction is 5.6 billion, your land acquisition backlog is 1.2 billion, your annual operations deficit is 400 million, and we are here talking about increasing fees to go into parks by $36 million, I think it has been pointed out that is kind of like a shot in the ocean, in trying to find the remaining shot.

The question that I have is that if we continue to go forward authorizing these great things out of this committee, and you continue to support them, we are never going to catch up with 36 million bucks. In fact, as you I am sure will agree, the minute you begin either to impose an entry fee into a park or you increase one, you have the public at your throat.

So the question is who can we blame? If Congress authorizes it, we blame Congress. But if the park's operational officer does it, we blame the Parks Department and we hang him out to dry.

So the question to me is, I think the priority here, what are we doing this for? We are going to anger a lot of people in this country with 36 million bucks, there is no question about it, whether it be in Hawaii or Oregon or Minnesota.

Is it worth the effort to gain $36 million to take the wrath of the public and then do nothing about the backlog, or do nothing about what people believe and perceive is going to be an improvement that their increased fees are going to provide for? Tell me what you think.

Mr. KENNEDY. I think about that, sir, that the public is already paying fees in lots of places but under a peculiar hodgepodge of rules which taken in the aggregate don't really provide a sense that everybody is providing a fair share in kind of an evenhanded way. These things have arrived. Pay it here. Don't pay it here. This exception. That exception. This much here. That much there.

It doesn't feel fair, and it also doesn't feel fair to a whole lot of people that the fees they pay don't stay in the parks. That just doesn't feel fair to people.

So, what we are trying to do is to provide for fairness across the board. Somebody's got to be responsible for setting out a system that is evenhanded with some rules that make pretty good sense that apply everywhere, to the extent that you can collect everywhere, which you can't, practically.

And secondly, that when somebody comes up to the gate and pays down a fee, most people think that is going to go help the park, and most of it doesn't. And that is not fair.

So I think, sir, that with regard to the general public's feeling, your feeling, my feeling, when we go to the place, this is a good piece of legislation. It is a piece of legislation that we can all support.

Now, it is true too that—sorry. Two more sentences, if I may.

There are two or three other provisions in this bill that are very important aside from the fee part of it and about which there tends to be pretty general assent. I just didn't want that to get lost in the discussion about fees.

Mr. SMITH. Well, thank you. And I agree with you that this bill that sets aside money for the parks where they are collected is a great idea.

The question I have to you is a judgment of imposing $36 million, which against a billion is quite insignificant. But you are still going to increase the wrath of the public the minute you do it, and they are going to want to know, "What is my increased fee doing for the park condition?"

Mr. KENNEDY. That is right. And that is exactly——

Mr. SMITH. That is the question.

Mr. KENNEDY. That is the core of our discussion. As it is, if you and I were going to try to stand in front of a bunch of people who have just waited in line for 3 hours to get into a park, and they just paid their fees, and we could say, "Guess what? What you just did, stand in line or sitting in your car sweltering, didn't go to take care of that park at all," I think there would be a lot of outrage. And we are just trying to fix that.

Mr. SMITH. Well, I applaud you for that. My question was the judgment of putting $36 million of increased fees in the bill.

Mr. KENNEDY. Oh.

Mr. SMITH. That is the question I had.

Mr. KENNEDY. If, as Mr. Vento suggested earlier, if we could put a, add another decimal point, we would be just delighted. But it doesn't look to us as if either we could do that or we get——

Mr. SMITH. I am suggesting eliminating it, not putting any more decimal points.

Mr. KENNEDY. I understand that, sir. And we are arguing we would like more.

Mr. SMITH. The other question I had is simply are you going to be this year coming before this committee supporting increases, or bills that increase the park's acquisition program, that increase construction, that increase areas that you are obviously terribly, terribly underfunded? Are you going to ask for new additions?

Mr. KENNEDY. You spoke of construction. I certainly hope we will in the next budget cycle be asking for money to——

Mr. SMITH. On the new land acquisition.

Mr. KENNEDY. New land acquisition. I guess we will have to look at those one by one, which is the way we conventionally do it. We think this belongs in the park system or don't we.

There is a bill before you which we support which will help us respond to your question by looking carefully at the criteria within which additions would be made with you. There is good legislation about that. That can help us avoid helter-skelter additions, and we support that legislation.

Mr. SMITH. The question directly then to you, you supported the chairman's heritage program, which was $35 million, and you have this huge backlog. How can you possibly support new additions when you can't meet your annual operation program?

Mr. KENNEDY. The chairman's heritage program doesn't call for additions to the parks. It calls for activity that would help other people not in the parks to do things that would produce for the public generally——

Mr. SMITH. It costs $35 million.

Mr. KENNEDY. That is money—but it is not an addition, for additions to the parks.

Mr. SMITH. But it is out of your budget?

Mr. KENNEDY. Well, but it is in addition to. It is a consequence of having certain—yes, you bet.

Mr. SMITH. It certainly has. Therefore, you are adding to the deficit again that you have already accumulated over the years. It wasn't yours. It has been going on for years. I am not suggesting—I am not blaming you. I am just commiserating with you——

Mr. KENNEDY. No, I know. And we thank you for your courtesy.

Mr. SMITH [continuing]. About the question of, you know, where are we coming from? Are we ever going to get a hold of this issue, or are we going to just keep adding new additions, carving out more money from your already overspent budget? And you are supporting it.

Mr. KENNEDY. Yes, sir.

Mr. SMITH. That is my problem.

Mr. KENNEDY. We are. We are supporting at once legislation which would provide other ways than additions to the National Park System to serve the purposes, the general purposes of the American public, take care of areas that need being attended to.

That will cost us some money, but not nearly as much money, nor as much difficulty, as would be the case if we were to add those places to the park system. That is the first thing.

The second thing is, of course, we are here to testify seeking more revenue that sticks within the parks.

Mr. SMITH. Well, you whipped out $35 million for the chairman's bill. Now you want to increase fees for $36 million which is going to enrage the public.

Mr. KENNEDY. We, I think, have a little difference of view as to what is more enraging. We think, sir, the unfairness in its not staying in the park is fairly enraging too.

Mr. SMITH. We should have let the people going into parks vote on Mr. Vento's bill. They likely would not have passed it if they thought it was going to increase their fees to go into the park just to pay for his heritage program.

Mr. KENNEDY. Well, Mr. Smith, I don't want to belabor this point with you, but it does seem to me that if we let—and I am serious about this, and I am not trying to be captious. If we were to let the people who were coming into parks vote on whether or not the fees they pay now—

Mr. SMITH. Oh, no. I am not suggesting that.

Mr. KENNEDY. Sure—should stick in the parks or not——

Mr. SMITH. I do know how they would vote. The question is they are not going to vote for any fees, obviously.

Well, I would like to help you set aside more fees for parks. I would like to do that. I just question the judgment of putting in $36 million.

Mr. VENTO. Let me thank the gentleman, and I won't get into a rhetorical argument. I did want to indicate that broadly I think there is support. Obviously, with the caveat that we try to, again, tie the resources raised, the entrance, the user, the other permit fees, to the park.

Mr. Frampton, I did want to give you an opportunity. I really much appreciate your being here.

But there are elements of this bill—everything being said, we are going to do something on fees in the committee. We are going to work with you to accomplish that. But there is a lot of trepidations about it, as you can see.

But there are the other aspects to the bill. Did you want to comment on these other aspects, Mr. Frampton?

I know that you had been working on them in the sense that you are talking about enhancing the ability to collect donations, the recovery for damages that occur in the park, trying to retain those dollars.

I first learned of this when working near St. Croix and talking to then Superintendent Finley of Everglades. We were talking about the reef that was damaged by a tour boat anchor. They collected money but couldn't keep the dollars. They went to the Treasury rather than back to the park.

And there is another aspect too of this particular effort. Did you want, before you leave, to comment about those three elements? I know you have to go.

Mr. FRAMPTON. Well, I would just like to say, Mr. Chairman, we are very eager to find more flexible ways, more effective ways of seeking private sector and local government partnership in supporting things that need to be done in and around the parks.

I realize that there is concern out there that you are going to drive up to Yosemite or Oregon Caves and see a big neon sign that says, "Brought to you by Coca-Cola." And we are very aware of the kinds of guidelines and criteria and discipline that is going to have to be developed to convince Members of Congress that this is something that can be done in a way that has integrity for the park system.

But the specific provisions, the challenge cost share program and the ability which we don't now have, except through the Park Foundation, and that is often cumbersome, to do private partnerships, that is what we are after here.

Just to give you an example from my own travels last week, we are working closely with the city of Estes Park, Colorado, to try to figure out a way that the Park Service, the Forest Service and the city can jointly build some deed-restricted, affordable housing in town, in Estes Park, on land that the city would buy with bonds through its Housing Authority, but that would provide affordable housing for Park Service employees outside of the park.

These are the kinds of creative things that are all win-win, have very few risks for the parks and the park system, that we need to be pioneering. And we don't have all the mechanisms to do that right now.

And the cost share provisions and the authority to accept donations into Park Service directly are two important vehicles for doing that.

And again, you know, if there are concerns here, this is not a, you know, we have the one and only solution. We are very eager to work with you and with members of the committee to try to shape something that makes sense and that gives people confidence that we are not, you know, undermining the integrity of the system here.

Mr. VENTO. Well, we are very concerned about any type of commercialization or what the commercialization degree would be. Obviously, we have taken some steps in the concession bill on that.

But I know that Chairman Miller is also interested in the activation of the Foundation. He has repeatedly mentioned that to me.

The other issue, of course, of permitting or activating the employees of the park to, in fact, obtain donations, to go out and set up appropriate programs for donations, is there some model that we can look to outside, other land management agencies or others, that are actually involved in that that could help us?

Mr. KENNEDY. Yes, sir.

Mr. VENTO. If you have to leave, Mr. Frampton, I don't want to—please.

Yes, Director Kennedy?

Mr. KENNEDY. The Smithsonian institution has a lot of experience along those lines, working within guidelines that protect both taste and the integrity of the institution. They have been at it a long time and it is not a new idea.

It is just that the—nor is it, in fact, a new idea for Park Service employees. They are out there doing it now.

We are just trying to endorse that. And once again, trying to give it a system by reference to other institutions, of which I suppose the most noticeable is the Smithsonian, with regard to how you do it safely and carefully.

Mr. VENTO. And finally, of course, this issue of vandalism and park resource damage that occurs and the dollars go to the Federal Treasury. What type of money are we talking about here on an annual basis? Do you have any figure? Mr. Finley?

Mr. FINLEY. Mr. Chairman, we don't have any figures, but I think the cumulative impacts would be very important to the parks. Just let me give you a couple of examples.

Let's take automobile accidents taking out old stone walls along—historic rock walls, or taking out gates, these types of things. Right now if you—currently, you send out park crews, you pay the materials, you pay the wages, those are lost from your budget. They are diverted from other tasks.

Mr. VENTO. And the money is paid to the Treasury.

Mr. FINLEY. That is right.

Mr. VENTO. So it would be a way. It seems that there is almost a constant problem with money in this way not coming back to the Park Service. It would be good, to get some numbers on these.

I understand that most of it is really an update of permitting the parks, if we want philanthropy and if we want an ability to partnership with local communities.

You talked about employee housing. As you know, Mr. Frampton, we have an outstanding meeting that we have to conclude on that issue.

One other matter I wanted to touch on, and I don't—Assistant Secretary Frampton, if you need to leave, please excuse yourself.

Mr. FRAMPTON. Thank you, Mr. Chairman.

Mr. VENTO. Thank you very much for being here. We appreciate it.

One other thing I wanted to call to my colleague's attention was, first of all—there are two issues, actually. One was this reservation system issue, Director Kennedy, that you want to talk about, which I think you instituted, and I may have a comment or two on that.

Mr. KENNEDY. Yes.

Mr. VENTO. And then secondly is the issue of the permit activity or activities, as an example, in the proposal that was before me with regards to Yellowstone. You might want to specifically talk about this permit activity, retaining the funds or charging extra dollars, plus, of course, what almost appeared to be like a fishing license type of issue in Yosemite.

The only reason I raise this is I don't know if you want us to deal with it in the context of this legislation. But I do want to talk about the reservation system issue——

Mr. KENNEDY. Yes. Thank you, sir.

Mr. VENTO [continuing]. And the other at this time.

Mr. KENNEDY. Mr. Finley is the resident expert on special uses in parks.

Would you speak to that, Mr. Finley?

Mr. FINLEY. Mr. Chairman, the special park use legislation before you provides a good opportunity for us to work with you on the authorities. Currently on special park uses we focus on cost recovery.

In other words, when we work with movies on locations or we do a permitting system such as we are doing in Yellowstone, it is really a cost recovery for the establishment of the permit system, the management of the permit system—the mailing, the filing, the cumulation of data, and the monitoring, and the enforcement of a permitting system.

Cost recovery is an important aspect to us. But more importantly, under this legislation should you choose to consider value would be just as important. That a special park use authority consider value and cost returned to the United States.

And, for example, a part of "Maverick" was filmed in Glen Canyon National Recreation Area. These types of industries—movie, cellular phones using existing radio antennas, not that we are going to put cellular phone antennas up, but we are approached by cellular phone companies, for example, and asked to use our existing antennas.

Well, right now we can't really do a recovery based on value. We have to say, "Well, that is the cost to the United States?" That is a loss. In terms of movie, they budget for location fees, but we currently are limited to charging for the cost of monitoring the resource damage, policing their activities.

Mr. VENTO. So, you are not really dealing with the fair market value.

Mr. KENNEDY. Not at all.

Mr. VENTO. You are just dealing with your cost, and so it may be low, it may be high, but it is——

Mr. KENNEDY. It is a missed opportunity, Mr. Chairman.

Mr. VENTO. Yes. Well, I understand that.

I think, also, of course, you want to talk about other individual park units—those individuals that would be visitors that would be using the park might have the same sort of phenomena affect them. Is it the intent to have that apply to other types of activities that go on that would reflect other factors?

Mr. FINLEY. The intent would be to look at anything other than the recreational aspect covered by camping. You would look at weddings, special events.

Mr. VENTO. I think it is very helpful. Other than recreational uses I think is very helpful to me because it would exclude—I have this vested interest in fishing, you understand.

Mr. FINLEY. Well, let me comment on that, Mr. Chairman. We would like to work with you. We would propose that we certainly would not institute a charge for fishing in areas where there are State licenses.

But, as you remember, we have six or seven areas where by legislation—not by legislation, by cession of jurisdiction, the States do not and cannot assess a fishing license. For example, Isle Royale.

Mr. VENTO. And so you are suggesting that maybe there ought to be an imposition of something other than simply a use. Well, that does in that sense make some sense.

Director Kennedy, did you have any further comments on this reservation system? Or are you going to yield to Mr. Finley for that?

Mr. KENNEDY. No. I think I will take this one.

Mr. VENTO. I wanted to point these out because I want them on the record.

Mr. KENNEDY. Yes.

Mr. VENTO. You know, in terms of members. You know they are not here today. But this is a very important aspect, this issue that Mr. Finley raised.

Mr. KENNEDY. Yes. I think this one I will have to take the responsibility for because I think it is a necessary and desirable recognition that in many of the most important places under our governance there are today cruel circumstances in which elderly people and others for whom it may not be so easy to stand in the wind or the rain, waiting for 2 or 3 hours in long lines to get into places when that really isn't what you do when you go to the ball game or go to the theater or go anywhere else.

That you can call an 800 number and make a reservation, if you are sitting in Hawaii or in St. Paul and you aren't just up for standing in the rain in Washington. When you happen to get into town to want to go to the Washington Monument there is just no way for you to know that some number of you are going to be able to be sure when you can get in.

Whereas anybody else who didn't want to try for that kind of reservation can stand in line if they want to. It isn't that you want anybody to have to make a reservation. It is just that some stipulated number of people who gain access can make a reservation to do so.

Now, we want to inch our way, if we were authorized to do so, if Congress thought it were a good idea to try to take care of people so that they could lay some plans when they come to Washington or to other places where there is a problem of getting in. If the Congress were to say to us, tell us—"Why don't you take two or three and see how it works and tell us about it," we would like to do that.

My own impression is that right now we are accumulating a set of disappointed Americans who want to go to the Washington Monument, and many parts of the year they just can't stand the gaff of waiting for it, and we need to make provision for that.

It is also true that it isn't altogether easy to get on the boat sometimes to get to the Statue of Liberty or Ellis Island because you stand in line an awful lot. And there are reservation systems that are possible for that now.

Once again, I reiterate, if you want to go to a ball game you don't have to do that. And I just think we should move our way slowly, carefully toward a reservation system. We do have telephones these days and do that kind of thing. We don't want to do it all at once.

Mr. VENTO. The association, though, in terms of members, as an example of one model that you developed would be about $10 per family to get reservations. A family of four to get reservations, a little less than that, to get reservations at, for instance, the Washington Monument.

Mr. KENNEDY. Yes, sir. There is no intention to collect a fee here. We are just trying to pay for the cost of doing it.

Mr. VENTO. It pays for the cost. So, I think it is important for members to understand that. I would think the Washington Monument, if there is any difficulty in terms of doing that, that there would be a small horde that would come to the Hill and let their Representatives and Senators know that there is a concern.

I would suggest, looking at that very carefully. I think it is an indication of the type of pressure in terms of limited use and elevators and other types of crunch points where you can't use it and something orderly would be helpful. Even the White house and the President, reservation number one, is a unit of the park system. So there is elaborate systems there and they have yet ended up with this first come, first served at a certain point with regards to the use of it.

So I don't know. You are going down a road where there are some examples of it, but probably not as well understood. But there is still access on an ad hoc basis.

On the other hand, there are other systems, like the Smithsonian for viewing their films or doing other things, where you can pick up a ticket and go to a show at a certain time of the day.

Mr. KENNEDY. Yes, sir.

Mr. VENTO. And it is much less in terms of cost. I think that something of that nature first.

Mr. KENNEDY. Mr. Chairman, I know you don't want to give a lot of time to this. There is one little distinction that occurs to one if one has been in both contexts.

One is that if you are waiting for the Imax Theater at the Air and Space Museum you are standing inside. And it makes a big difference if you are standing out there in the heat in August in Washington and you are 85 years old.

Mr. VENTO. No, I agree. But I think that there is a system of organizing it so you know that you are going to go at a certain time or you are going to do something——

Mr. KENNEDY. Sure.

Mr. VENTO [continuing]. And you don't have the sort of phenomena of standing. So I think it is something on a pilot basis that is okay to do. As I said to you, I don't know that your doing it at the Washington Monument is the best idea because of the sort of lightning rod effect that the Washington Monument has on the Hill. So I would think I would want to institute that someplace else to work it out, myself.

But, if you want to get into that kind of challenge, I commend you for it.

But I wanted to point these out to my colleagues. I have a lot of other questions. I am not going to ask them.

Congresswoman Mink, did you have further questions at this time?

Mrs. MINK. I just have one question about the fees for commercial activities in the parks such as the movie companies that come out to shoot volcano scenes. Is there any current practice or authority for charging these companies for the use of the park scenery and hazarding their own lives in the course of it, and when a catastrophe happens, engaging all the emergency services of the county and the State to rescue them? Is there a bond authority already given to the Park Service to protect the parks and the State and county government from such activity?

And the outrageous behavior of the last company is beyond understanding.

Mr. KENNEDY. Pieces of that question, if I may try them in sequence. There is a current system which gets you cost recovery and nothing else. Cost recovery, very limited.

Second, with regard to insurance, yes. But I don't believe, and Mr. Finley I don't think believes either, that we are currently protecting other people's interests. I am sure the insurance process takes care of some of that, but I would be surprised if it took care of enough of it, Congresswoman.

Mrs. MINK. Does your pending legislation cover that adequately, the costs that could be incurred by the other governmental authorities with reference to a——

Mr. KENNEDY. The regulations that would follow from our legislation would indeed do exactly that. We want to be sure that everybody gets it back and a little more, because you are not going to get—if you just cost it out, really what it is going to cost you.

And also—sorry—there was another part of your question too which is important and needs an answer. As it is, of course, the superintendent doesn't give permits, or shouldn't, when there is any damage to the essential resources of the place. However, you have referred to an instance of which I am also pointedly aware in which the provision or the admission was not responsibly followed by the private party, perhaps, and we need to police that too.

Mrs. MINK. Are you able to assess fines where they violate the conditions of the permit?

Mr. KENNEDY. Yes. But I believe also that in the—there is a previous instance here where if you do something awful and it costs you a lot of money, it goes to the general revenues, and that doesn't help you in the park.

Mr. VENTO. Is that the fine money—pardon me. If the gentlewoman would yield?

Mrs. MINK. Yes, I yield.

Mr. VENTO. Does the fine dollars also go to the—of course, that goes, that is a judicial determination, so that is not retained; is that correct?

Mr. KENNEDY. Yes, sir.

Mr. VENTO. Your intention here is to, in the third provision—if the gentlewoman will continue to yield—on lawsuits where there is damage to the resource or fines that they would then be retained by the park?

Mr. KENNEDY. Yes, sir.

Mr. VENTO. That is fairly unusual. I would think that the fine issue especially is, but the OMB and the Administration has, in fact——

Mr. KENNEDY. Oh, I beg your pardon. I am corrected. I gather not the fines for technical reasons. And you are quite correct.

Mr. VENTO. I would think that that would be a problem.

Mr. KENNEDY. Yes, sir.

Mr. VENTO. Do you have further questions?

Mrs. MINK. No, that is it. Thank you.

Mr. VENTO. Congressman Smith?

Mr. SMITH. Mr. Chairman, you raised the special park uses issue, and I want to ask Director Kennedy, the language provides that the fees shall cover all costs of providing necessary services. Since the Parks Department is not compelled to provide efficiencies or isn't directed to contain costs, are you sure you are not strapping yourself into eliminating a whole bunch of services?

Because when you attach all your costs, my friend, we might not be able to go there and use these parks for special services.

Mr. KENNEDY. A movie company comes in, wants to use the place, we would under this provision tell them everything it is going to cost us. And then if they don't want to buy in on that basis, good-bye.

I have shot a few movies in parks, and the current fees are just absurdly low, because they don't really cover, and movie companies are frequently quite capable, even television companies who are paying—they pay a lot every place else for the access to the place, they just don't pay much when they get to the National Parks. So this is a kind of equity provision. Let's get these people to pay something like what they would pay if they shot it somewhere else.

Mr. VENTO. I wonder if—the gentleman would yield.

Mr. SMITH. Yes, I yield.

Mr. VENTO. If we would be better off just saying that a fair market value is what they would pay some place else, unless that language would be too confusing.

Mr. KENNEDY. No, sir.

Mr. VENTO. I think Congressman Smith's point in terms of trying to—it seems to me to put a burden on you to come with trying to articulate all of these costs and lead you down a rule and regulation and a lot of commotion, whereas if we just had something like fair market value, there is a lot of flexibility in that.

Mr. KENNEDY. Well, we welcome that suggestion. I guess Mr. Finley suggests that I amend that response by saying and cost too.

Mr. VENTO. Well, I think you can always use—in actually using the cost. In other words, you want to have something that is tangible. I think just giving you absolute flexibility in that case is the instance, I suspect, if the gentleman would continue to yield, that there has been a benefit to the park. By having film companies in to share the splendor of the Grand Canyon and put it into a film, it is not a bad thing for the park.

Mr. KENNEDY. No, it is not.

Mr. VENTO. So there is a tangential benefit here that does take place besides the film.

Mr. DUNCAN.

I assume that, Mr. Smith, you have concluded.

Mr. SMITH. Yes.

Mr. DUNCAN. Just a couple of questions, Mr. Chairman.

Director Kennedy, do you think that these interest fees would be more in the line of setting fees where there are no fees now, or would the places where there are fees now be likely to increase?

Mr. KENNEDY. The fees that would get you up to the $30-odd million would be very slight increases of a buck on five, that kind of thing. You don't have to do it a lot to get there, and you would indeed hope to get most of what you are going to get by making it fairly distributed across the system. That is about what you are doing.

Mr. DUNCAN. Where you have fees now, or do you envision when you set up these fees any exclusion for lower income people?

Mr. KENNEDY. Yes, sir, there are a bunch of exclusions or modifications or reductions, pretty much what you have got now in the structure. There are no radical shifts in that, just the percentages a little bit, but these are all on margin. There is no substantial change in the pattern as it is now, no substantial one. There are some adjustments.

Mr. DUNCAN. What is the pattern now? Let's say if you have a person who qualifies for an earned income tax credit on the income tax return. Do they get some kind of card or slip or something?

Mr. FINLEY. No, Congressman. The current exemptions under exiting law are targeted to the following groups. You would have individuals under 16 years of age are exempt from a recreational fee; you would have the disabled under the provisions of the disability; you would have the Golden Age provision for a benefit by provision of age over 62; you would have the exemption for a bona fide educational institution. In other words, when you bring a bus of school kids from a high school or a grade school, they are not charged a recreational fee. There is a therapeutic waiver, in other words, a bona fide—like Saint Elizabeth's or something like that where you would bring some patients for therapeutic purposes to parks; they are excluded.

Now specifically to your question of low income, there are no specific provisions, but there are opportunities such as free days where the director of the National Park Service and various park units waive fees on certain days of the year which would accommodate that aspect. In the urban areas where many people may fit that category, we have areas that are administratively not feasible to charge fees because of multiple entrances and so forth.

So while there is no specific category based on an income exclusion or level, there are a multitude of other categories or opportunities that exist.

Mr. DUNCAN. Do you have any type of reduced rate for people who are frequent users?

Mr. FINLEY. Yes, sir. For example—I'll give you an example of Everglades National Park and Yosemite National Park. For your frequent users, let's say a fisherperson at the Everglades who lives in Miami, there is currently a $15 annual permit. That equates to about $1.25 a month or 4 cents a day that you can have recurrent access to the park.

There is also the provision of the annual Golden Eagle which is currently $25. That allows you entrance to all units of the National Park System and some Forest Service units or other Federal fee areas. That equates prorated to about two dollars a month or six cents a day.

So there are currently some avenues that we would propose to raise a little bit, as the director said, on the margin. Initially we would propose to raise the Golden Eagle from $25 a year to $35 a year, but, again, if you prorate those, those still provide reasonable access for locals at a very low rate.

Mr. DUNCAN. All right.

Thank you very much.

Mr. VENTO. Congresswoman Mink is going to, I appreciate, take over. I have Congressman de Lugo's statement here, and predictably I think that members for many reasons are concerned about the prospect of raising the fee or having an entrance fee in their park. In this case he points out, properly so, that the philanthropy that provided for the designation of the park was a trust from apparently one of the great philanthropic families of the country and feels that there shouldn't be a fee. So I think we are going to have this differential system.

This general authority that you seek logically is something that we are going to have to pull back on and look at urban areas and look at this, I understand, and we want to work on that. So I think unless there are compelling reasons, I think we are going to keep control over amounts and locations.

I will put Congressman de Lugo's statement in the record.

[Prepared statement of Mr. De Lugo follows:]

Statement of
the Hon. Ron de Lugo
before the Subcommittee on
National Parks, Forests and Public Lands
hearing on H.R. 4533
June 10, 1994

Thank you Mr. Chairman for giving me the opportunity to make an opening statement today. Let me also welcome Director Kennedy back to the subcommittee, once again, and to let him know that I look forward to hearing his testimony today as I always do.

As you know Mr. Chairman, I am among the strongest supporters of maintaining and enhancing our National Parks system in this committee and the Congress as a whole. Along with our former committee Chairman, Mo Udall, as well as other members such as yourself, our current full committee Chairman, Mr. Miller, our late colleague Phil Burton and the former Chairman of this subcommittee, John Seiberling, we have together supported and voted in favor of the establishment of many of the National Parks that currently are in existence today.

I am very proud of this accomplishment. There is, however, one sad fact which seem always to spoil the great record of our national parks: and that is the inability of the parks to receive the funding they need to be maintained and operated as the world class attractions that they are.

It is this problem of the lack of adequate funding for our national parks, which the bill before us today, H.R. 4533, seeks to address. While I applaud the efforts of Secretary Babbitt and Director Kennedy in recognizing the need for finding a solution to this problem, I must state clearly my strong objections to the particular solution that is proposed by H.R. 4533, because of its potential impact upon the Virgin Islands National Park in my District.

Mr. Chairman, the Virgin Islands National Park was established in 1956, after Mr. Laurance S. Rockefeller donated over 5,000 acres to the federal government to establish a national park on St. John. In 1978, Public Law 95-348 was enacted as an amendment to the 1956 law which established the park, to provide that "no fee or charge shall be imposed for entrance or admission into the Virgin Islands National Park".

I wish to note, Mr. Chairman, that it has come to my attention that all reference to Mr. Laurance Rockefeller's donation of the land to establish the Virgin Islands National park has been removed from literature that is given to visitors to the park. I find this action deplorable and should not be allow to continue. Not only because it is an insult to Mr. Rockefeller generosity, but because it should be National Park policy to honor such donations in order to encourage others to make similar contributions so that we can begin to clear up the tremendous backlog in land acquisitions that our parks are facing today. I believe that instead of de-emphasizing Mr. Rockefeller's important contribution to the Virgin Islands National Park, we should erect a plaque to honor him so that others may know and remember the love that he and others like him share towards preserving our nations treasures for future generations.

If the bill before us is enacted, it would give the Secretary of Interior the very broad authority to impose a per-person entrance fee at whichever national park unit he deems appropriate, including the Virgin Islands National Park. If an entrance fee were to ever be imposed a the V.I. Park, it would mean that the "trust" that was established between the federal government and the people of the Virgin Islands in Public Law 95-348, that Virgin Islands National Park will always be free of the imposition of entrance fees, would be broken.

The Virgin Islands National Park, Mr. Chairman, is a park that exists on an island within a local community. There are multiple access areas to the park, including many boat entrances and public roads which go through the Park. There is not just one main entrance. It is therefore unlikely, in any case, that a fee could be collected at a unit like St. John without a main entrance.

While I fully support and appreciate the goal of H.R. 4533, I am afraid that I would not be able to support its enactment into law if doing so would mean that the residents of the island of St. John, which the Virgin Islands National Park comprises two-thirds of, could not enjoy the beaches and other areas of their native island, as they have done for centuries, without having to pay an entrance fee.

Thank you again, Mr. Chairman, for giving me an opportunity to make this brief opening statement. I look forward to working with you and Director Kennedy to continue to try to resolve the problem of the lack of adequate funding for our national parks. I do not believe, however, that giving the Secretary of Interior broad authority to impose entrance fees, especially at Parks where imposing entrance fees is prohibited by current law, is the solution.

Mr. VENTO. Secondly, I want to point out that I favor many of the changes you are talking about. Eliminating the per vehicle charge is a big deal. So if you put an individual charge on everyone in the vehicle, it is going to be a different ball game in terms of what is raised here, and I think we ought to proceed with that and recognize that.

Thirdly, the idea of the Golden Age pass and what was happening where you have a carload of people and, because I am 65 and have a Golden Age pass which exempts me into the park forever, everyone in the car gets to come in, my grandchildren that are 29 years old, as an example.

So I think there has been really a prejudice, a proper prejudice I think, in terms of trying to expand and to engage and to bring people in. I think we are at a point now where we can talk about reasonable fees for others.

We want to do what we should do by the terms of someone having earned that Golden Age pass, and I haven't earned it yet, but I would note that the AARP has been sending me applications for a couple of years. In any case, they start rather early.

Mrs. MINK. They start at age 50.

Mr. VENTO. Yes, they start at a younger age than they should perhaps.

Mr. KENNEDY. We will welcome you, Mr. Chairman, when you are ready for it.

Mr. VENTO. It may take 15 years to convince me.

So I want the record and the members to be aware of these, because I think that, candidly, they are the sorts of things that can engender some discussion and perhaps some controversy, as Congressman Smith said. But I think, frankly, the overwhelming majority of the people that are interested in parks are willing to pay the fees.

I don't think there has been maybe sharing, but we have a lot of urban parks even in the Washington area that do have some fees associated with them. It is not just a collection of the fee, but it is a way to regulate and to regularize what is happening there to ensure the presence and to provide for interpretation; someone collecting a fee is not merely just collecting a fee, not if they are doing their job the way I think that we intended it to be done. So I intend to work on this.

Obviously, we are not going to give the administration all the flexibility that they want and in most instances probably can justify, but I think there has been a history of concern, as is indicated here in just one instance, and I think as we go around to the park systems you will find the same sort of phenomena.

But I don't think that has made for quite the eclectic response. I do think it makes sense on an individual basis, and that is why I started out by saying I understand the sentiments of the individual superintendents and why they respond the way they do to entrance and user fees. We have to recognize that, and I think Director Kennedy, in trying to get off the dime of a very tough question from my colleague from Wyoming and others, a tough questions in terms of why we don't collect it—I do think the superintendents need that ability to finally make that decision, how long they are going to keep someone at the entrance point or they are not?

We want to try to provide the incentives so that at least there are some dollars retained in the park, their expenses at least are partially offset by virtue of it, and I think we have made some progress last year, and I hope we can, with the cooperation of all my colleagues on the committee, go forward.

But I know I am not going to be able to obtain that unless I recognize the specific idiosyncracies that, in fact, are quite justified in some of these instances in the Virgin Islands and Hawaii and other areas. But I think we can march forward and hopefully put a finish on this so it isn't back up here again next year, and I think we have gone a long way, but it is going to take some good faith effort to get it done.

With that said, I want to thank Congresswoman Mink. I won't be able to stay here for the next panel. I know the National Parks and Conservation Association have put a lot of work into their testimony, as has Susan Henley, a good friend with the American Hiking Society, but I want to go to the Floor and see if I can try to persuade my colleagues to work on the California Desert measure.

So I want to thank you.

If there are further questions Congresswoman Mink may have for the panel——

Mrs. MINK. Thank you, Mr. Chairman.

Mr. VENTO. I want to thank her.

PANEL CONSISTING OF PHILIP H. VOORHEES, WASHINGTON REPRESENTATIVE, NATIONAL PARKS AND CONSERVATION ASSOCIATION; AND, SUSAN A. HENLEY, VICE PRESIDENT, AMERICAN HIKING SOCIETY

Mrs. MINK [presiding]. Any further comments to this panel? If not, the chair will call the next panel to the witness table, and without objection all of the opening statements that have been prepared by members of the committee will be inserted in the record.

Mr. Phil Voorhees, the Washington representative of National Parks and Conservation Association, and Ms. Susan Henley, vice president of the American Hiking Society, if they will come toward forward to the table, Mr. Voorhees first.

STATEMENT OF PHILIP H. VOORHEES

Mr. VOORHEES. Thank you, Madam Chairman.

My name is Phil Voorhees. I am a Washington representative of the National Parks and Conservation Association.

Most of the major points of our both concern and support for this legislation have been covered in the past hour and a half of this hearing, so I will go over only briefly the major points of my written statement and ask——

Mrs. MINK. Thank you. That will be fine. The entire statement will be inserted in the record at this point.

Mr. VOORHEES. Thank you very much.

It has been apparent to NPCA, as it has been apparent to users of the National Parks, that the current system of setting, collecting, and administering entrance and user fees is cumbersome, haphazard, and clearly inadequate. As a member organization, we regularly receive letters and queries from our members asking why no attendant was available to collect the entrance fee on their last trip to the parks. We also receive a substantial amount of mail asking why visitors are made to pay to enter some parks and not others. Both of these are quite legitimate questions, and they are hard questions to answer under the current system.

The legislation being considered today should be regarded as a first step toward restructuring the Park Service's fee program on a more rational basis.

There is a long history of a tug-o-war between Congress and the Department of the Interior on the authority to both set fees and manage the collection of the fee receipts going all the way back to 1908 when the first fees were accorded to automobile users at Mount Rainier National Park, I believe, and the authority was held essentially by the National Park Service, by the Department of the Interior, until 1918 when Representative John Fitzgerald of New York, then chairman of the Interior Appropriations Subcommittee, shelved Park Service Director Stephen Mather's plans to use all fee revenues that were brought into the system in the small number of parks that then collected the fees to replace military management at Yellowstone with civilian personnel. I think that point was mentioned by Director Kennedy, and it is a very valid point.

As the committee considers offering the NPS broader authority over collection and use of the fees, however, it should not lose sight of the fact that the public visitor is not the only visitor to—excuse me, not the only user of the parks. There are a substantial number of commercial users of the parks which are largely overlooked, it seems to me, to some extent now and certainly in past efforts since the Land and Water Conservation Act providing the current structure to the system was established in the mid-sixties.

These commercial users include air and bus tour companies, concessionaires, Hollywood production companies, as were mentioned before, oil, gas, and electric utilities who have lines crossing the parks, communications companies, commercial photographers, and a variety of other smaller users.

Despite the substantial revenues these firms generate by using the park resources, typically they pay very little or nothing back to the Federal Government, and, as I say, there have been few attempts to focus on this matter.

It seems to us that any new legislation should depart from requiring attempts to provide a fix to the fee system and specifically state that the commercial users of the National Parks who gain financial advantages from the use of the parks be considered first for any fee reviews and increases. The bill as currently written does include some very loose language stating that all fees shall be fair and equitable taking into consideration the benefits to the recipient.

The language, however, should be tightened up and made stronger, stating that it is the intent of the authors to consider untapped commercial users as the source of additional revenues first before the public is asked to pay additional monies.

It is clear, however, that more revenue can and should be generated from public users of the National Parks. As I said before, we get a substantial amount of mail on the issue, and just as many people ask not only why was there no one to collect my fees but why are the fees so low, so clearly there is a well of concern among the public that the fees need to be adjusted. In some ways perhaps they need to be adjusted downwards, in some ways they need to be adjusted upward.

It seems quite reasonable that the Park Service should have the authority to make those decisions and not have to come up to Congress periodically and quite regularly to review the matter and essentially beg for increases in specific individual parks.

Under the legislative proposal before you, the Park Service would be allowed to retain a portion of the fee receipts. In reconciliation last year, they were allowed to retain 15 percent of the collected revenue off the top to pay for the revenue collection. That has been reviewed earlier. Ample precedence exists, however, to allow the Park Service to retain all of the revenues generated through the fees.

As I mentioned, that was the genesis of the initial fee system. In fact, it was the assumption that the automobile permits that were first issued at Mount Rainier in 1908, that all such fees collected by the Park Service would be deposited and held in a special Treasury account similar to the one proposed as the National Park Renewal Fund and would be available to the Park Service directly without congressional appropriation.

As it is currently structured under the legislation, the National Park Renewal Fund will be filled with only a small portion of the total funds generated through entrance and user fees. According to the Park Service's projections for 1996, the first year the park renewal funds will be available, $46 million of the $170 million in projected total fee revenues would be directly available for use by the parks. Madam Chairman, it seems to us that that figure should be $170 million available directly to National Parks.

However, let me offer a caveat that no one should be misled into thinking that fees for the public users, commercial businesses, or any other special groups will ever provide a very significant portion of the total budget of the National Park Service.

Fee revenues, including concessions revenues, will generate perhaps $112 million or roughly 8.5 percent of the total budget in 1994. Even if the provisions of this legislation, H.R. 4533, and concessions reform legislation were to pass, and if the Park Service were to execute its plan to raise entrance fees, the Park Service would be fortunate to generate $200 million by 1997. By then the ratio of fees to total budget may have leapt to only about 14 percent.

What this demonstrates is that the maintenance of a viable National Park Service will always be the primary responsibility of the American taxpayer. To tinker with this system substantially and expect that you are going to gain a significant portion of the total revenues for the National Park Service budget through user and other fees risks a variety of very real problems, including who essentially are the ones who benefit from the parks, the individuals who are providing substantial fees as opposed to the general public, any corporate donors who are providing substantial fees as opposed to the general public.

It seems to us that the general public should always be regarded first since they will always be paying the substantial portion through their basic taxes.

In addition, it seems to us that as we move forward in considering a complete restructuring of the fee system, first and foremost, the Park Service should be required to do an economic study of the various users of the park resources, the costs of those uses, and any benefits derived by the user. Congress should require that such a study be completed within six months of passage to ensure that the Park Service is proceeding in the right direction. This study should also include input from park visitors.

It seems to us that the Park Service is reaching a little bit too far for complete authority over fees without any measurable amount of review on the part of Congress. It seems to us also reasonable then that the legislation should allow for a biennial review of entrance and user fees.

Now with respect to the issue of fund-raising, the second part of the legislation here, fund-raising already occurs at many parks but without the protection of any explicit authorization. To the extent that this is a reality, it is necessary and useful that this legislation provide that authority in some form. However, we urge that the committee proceed with due caution in the area.

Though the need for additional project-specific funds is clear in many parks, the risks associated with soliciting donations and structure cost share agreements are considerable. Simply put, private donors, whether they be corporations or foundations, usually want something in return, and by inviting private participation and funding of park projects, superintendents implicitly invite private donors to influence the Park Service's priorities.

I do not, however, mean to convey a position that private donations to the parks are bad, they are an increasingly necessary resource for individual parks and for the Park Service as a whole. As budget austerity continues to restrict the Park's ability to fund its priority projects, the topic of project-related fund-raising becomes an ever more critical concern and may warrant separate consideration from the issue of restructuring the National Park System fees.

In conclusion, let me say simply that more leeway is due for the Park Service to make its own fee decisions and is clearly warranted. But it is equally clear that some level of congressional and public oversight is also warranted. Periodic review of the fees levied to the National Park users and greater policy oversight of the prioritization of donor-financed projects may provide that level.

Congress and the Park Service should look upon this legislation as the first installment of a larger opportunity to plan carefully for the parks' needs and understand more deeply the public's expectations for how the parks should be funded. Director Kennedy should be commended for beginning the process by constructing this legislation.

That concludes my statement. Thank you very much.

[Prepared statement of Mr. Voorhees follows:]

National Parks
and Conservation Association

STATEMENT OF
PHILIP H. VOORHEES
NATIONAL PARKS AND CONSERVATION ASSOCIATION

BEFORE THE
SUBCOMMITTEE ON NATIONAL PARKS, FORESTS AND PUBLIC LANDS

ON HR 4533, THE NATIONAL PARK SERVICE ENTREPRENEURIAL MANAGEMENT REFORM ACT

JUNE 10, 1994

Mr. Chairman and members of the subcommittee, my name is Phil Voorhees. I am a Washington Representative for the National Parks and Conservation Association (NPCA), America's only private nonprofit citizen organization dedicated solely to protecting, preserving, and enhancing the U.S. National Park System.

On behalf of our Association, I am pleased to appear before the subcommittee to submit the Association's views on HR 4533, the National Park Service Entrepreneurial Management Reform Act. It has been apparent to NPCA, as it has been apparent to the users of the national parks, that the current system of setting, collecting, and administering entrance and user fees is cumbersome, haphazard, and clearly inadequate. We regularly receive letters and queries from our members asking why no attendant was available to collect the entrance fee on their last trip to the parks. We also receive mail asking why visitors are made to pay to enter some parks and not others. Both of these are very good questions, and they exemplify the confusion created by the current system. The legislation being considered today, HR 4533, should be regarded as the first step toward reconstructing the Park Service's fee program on a more rational basis.

HR 4533, however, is more than just a proposal to reform the fee system; it also includes language allowing park superintendents far broader authority to solicit donations and enter into challenge cost share agreements for the purposes of generating additional revenue for park projects. Park fees and park fund raising are two very different issues, and I will discuss them separately here.

1776 Massachusetts Avenue, N.W., Washington, D.C. 20036-1904
Telephone (202) 223-NPCA(6722) • Fax (202) 659-0650

National Park Service Fees

In HR 4533, the National Park Service is seeking broad authority to establish and adjust entrance and user fees and to expend the revenue for park purposes. As this committee well knows, there is a long history of a tug of war over this authority between the Park Service and Congress, dating back to 1918, when Rep. John Fitzgerald of New York, chairman of the Interior Appropriations subcommittee, shelved Stephen Mather's plans to use fee revenues to replace military management of Yellowstone with civilian personnel. In the last round of this struggle, in 1965, Congress affirmed its authority to set fees under the Land and Water Conservation Fund Act. Since that time, the National Park Service has returned to Congress nine times to request fee increases, eight times successfully. Clearly, this is a cumbersome process that severely limits the ability of the Park Service to make periodic necessary adjustments to both the level and the scope of fees.

As the committee considers offering the NPS broader authority over collection and use of fees, it should not lose sight of the fact that the public visitor is not the only user of the parks. A substantial number of private businesses use the parks and gain significant monetary advantage from that use. Such private users include concessioners; air and bus tour companies; Hollywood production companies; oil, gas, and electric utilities; communications companies; commercial photographers; and others. Despite the substantial revenues these firms generate by using park resources, typically they pay little or nothing back to the federal government. All nine attempts to raise fees since LWCF was passed, have focused on raising fees for the public, with little attention paid to commercial users.

Any new legislation should depart from prior attempts to provide a fix to the fee system and specifically state that commercial users of the national parks who gain financial advantages from use of the parks be considered first for fee reviews and increases. Although HR 4533 provides language stating that "all fees... shall be fair and equitable, taking into consideration... the benefits to the recipient," the bill should include stronger language stating that it is the intent of the authors to consider untapped commercial users as the source of additional revenues first. In this climate of fiscal austerity, every effort should be made to understand the cost of commercial and other special uses of the park and require full compensation of all NPS costs associated with these uses, including the cost of administation, additional law enforcement, security or other monitoring, and any other direct and indirect costs of the use.

With NPCA's support, Congress already has acknowledged the revenue potential of commercial users of the parks, first by imposing a separate access fee for commercial bus and some air tour operators in last year's budget reconciliation act and more recently by moving concessions reform legislation steadily through the legislative process toward final passage. The process begun in budget reconciliation and concessions legislation should be finished by including explicit statements of policy in new fee legislation.

Acknowledging the need for a higher level of contribution from private users, it is clear that more revenue can and should be generated from public users of the national parks as well. This legislation provides the Secretary with the authority to apply and adjust fees throughout the National Park System as the Secretary sees fit. The bill allows parks to retain 15 percent of the revenue to cover the cost of collection, and provides additional incentives for collection through the establishment of the "National Park Renewal Fund," which the Park Service could access directly without further appropriation. This is an admirable first step, but the bill does not go far enough.

Ample precedent exists to allow the Park Service to retain all of the revenues generated through fees. Indeed, it was on this assumption that automobile permits were first issued at Mt. Rainier in 1908. Until Rep. Fitzgerald's legislative prohibition on July 1, 1918, all such fees collected by the Park Service were deposited and held in a special Treasury account, similar to the proposed National Park Renewal Fund, and were available to the Park Service directly without congressional appropriation.

Superintendents have been lax about collecting entrance fees because they have seen no direct benefit from their collection and because collection of the funds placed an additional personnel burden on already slim resources. The 15 percent retention provision covers the drain on personnel resources. But the National Park Renewal Fund will be filled only with a small portion of the total funds generated through entrance and user fees. HR 4533 states that only 50 percent of the funds collected above the 1993 base level of fee collections would be available to NPS and the parks without congressional appropriation; the rest would move through the usual process of annual appropriation. According to the Park Service's projections for 1996 (the first year that Park Renewal Funds would be available), $36 million of the $170 million in projected total fee revenues would be directly available for use by the parks. Mr. Chairman, this figure should be $170 million.

No one should be misled into thinking that fees for the public users, commercial businesses, or any other special groups will ever provide a significant portion of the total budget of the National Park Service. In 1994, the NPS budget stands at approximately $1.3 billion. Fee revenues, including concession revenues, will generate perhaps $112 million, or roughly 8.5 percent of the budget. Even if HR 4533 and concessions reform legislation were to pass and if the Park Service were to execute its plan to raise entrance fees, the Park Service would be fortunate to generate $200 million by 1997. By then, the ratio of fees to total budget may have leapt to 14 percent. What this demonstrates is that maintenance of a viable national park system will always the primary responsibility of the American taxpayer. As the committee and the Park Service work to restructure the fee system, weighing proposals to change the structure of fee collection and to allow corporate participation in funding park initiatives and other departures from the current system, we should not lose sight of the limits to the potential of non-taxpayer financing of the parks, and the very real problems that any significant departure from this tradition may create.

Clearly, this risk argues for a more cogent plan and a well thought-out planning process for changing the fee system. HR 4533 reaches for the broadest possible authority and yet presents no such plan. To ensure that the National Park Service establishes for itself a sound basis for applying and periodically adjusting fees to both public and private users, the Park Service must proceed first with an economic study of the various users of the park resources, the cost of that use, and any benefit derived by the user. Congress should require that such a study be completed within six months of passage of this legislation to ensure that the Park Service is proceeding in the right direction. This study should also include input from park visitors. Only by better understanding the users of the parks can either Congress or the Park Service hope to achieve anything more than a haphazard system of fees and fee collection. Similarly, to ensure that the National Park Service's new fee system conforms with Congress's direction, the legislation should allow for a biennial review of entrance and user fees.

Project-Related Fundraising

Separate from additional authority on fees, HR 5433 seeks additional authority for park superintendents to raise funds and to enter into challenge cost share agreements for park projects. Fundraising at the park level already occurs at many parks, but without the protection of any explicit authorization. To the extent that this is a reality, it is necessary and useful that this legislation provide that authority in some form. However, we urge that the committee proceed with due caution in this area. Specifically, we believe the committee should require the Park Service to provide a far higher level of structure and accountability regarding which projects receive funding and under what conditions funding is provided.

As with restructuring the fee system, it may make sense to provide a higher level of authority and discretion for superintendents to raise funds for needed but chronically unfunded projects. NPCA just completed a survey of the national park superintendents, and the results clearly show that the most critically underfunded projects vary considerably from park to park, from decaying roads, to antiquated interpretive facilities, to dilapidated employee housing.

Though the need for additional project-specific funds is clear in many parks, the risks associated with soliciting donations and structuring cost share agreements are considerable. Simply put, private donors, whether they be corporations or foundations, usually want something in return, and by inviting private participation in funding park projects, superintendents implicitly invite private donors to influence the Park Service's priorities. Not only does this call into question the ability of the Park Service to structure its own priorities, it calls into question who benefits most from the donations: the public, who funds the vast majority of park activities, or the private donor.

Let me offer an example of our concern. In 1989, Mount Rushmore National Monument personnel began developing plans to expand visitor facilities and provide additional parking. Propelled by a pledge to fund the project by a local friends group, the Denver Service Center was brought in to develop a DCP for the project. When the DSC voiced opposition to the scope of the plan, the friends group contracted instead with a Denver architecture and engineering firm to do the work. The work is now proceeding at an estimated cost of $53 million, and the friends group has realized its inability to raise more than a small portion of the funds required.

The superintendent is now planning to ask the state of South Dakota to issue tax exempt bonds to cover the remaining cost for the parking facility, paying off the bond through a $4 to $5 per car parking fee. None of this planning was done on a centralized basis in the Park Service, and clearly, the $53 million might more wisely be spent on other projects. This example alone gives us pause when considering plans to allow even broader authority for superintendents to seek donor-funded projects.

I do not mean to convey a position that private donations to the parks are bad. They are an increasingly necessary resource for individual parks and for the Park Service as a whole. To ensure that park priorities are not compromised by cost share agreements or other project-related fundraising, this legislation should be considered carefully. As budget austerity continues to constrict the parks' ability to fund its priority projects, the topic of project-related fundraising becomes ever more critical and may warrant separate consideration from the issue of restructuring the National Park Service fee system. This policy should establish a structure to help superintendents resist donor-driven reprioritization of national park needs, and should set a hierarchy of priorities for funding as follows: first critical natural resource protection projects; then essential services such as decaying infrastructure and housing, and substandard interpretation; and, finally, management and amenity projects, providing new structures, additional access and the like.

Separate from the fee and fundraising portions of the legislation, HR 5433 contains language that allows the Park Service to receive insurance compensation for damage caused to the parks. Current federal policy demands that all such settlement funds be sent to the General Treasury, but the Park Service is responsible for providing the funding for repairs. This language resolves a long-standing inequity and is supported by NPCA.

Conclusion

HR 4533 is the first step in figuring out more appropriate, economically justifiable, and easier-to-administer fee and fund-raising policies for the National Park Service. More leeway for the Park Service to make its own fee decisions is clearly warranted, but it is equally clear that some level of congressional and public oversight is warranted. For both the issue of fees and project-related fundraising, the public has the right to know how the its money is being spent. Periodic review of the fees levied to national park users and greater policy oversight of the prioritization of donor-financed projects will provide that.

Congress and the Park Service should look upon this legislation as the first installment of a larger opportunity to plan more carefully for the parks' needs and understand more deeply the public's expectations for how the parks should be funded. Director Kennedy should be commended for beginning the process by constructing this legislation. NPCA looks forward to working with both the National Park Service and this committee to construct a more fair, balanced funding system for the national parks.

Mrs. MINK. Thank you, Mr. Voorhees.
Ms. Henley.

STATEMENT OF SUSAN A. HENLEY

Ms. HENLEY. Thank you, Mrs. Mink.

I represent the American Hiking Society. My name is Susan Henley, and I am the vice president. We are a national nonprofit organization. We have 118 club affiliates all around the country. Including our individual members, we represent about a half million people.

Our primary interest is trails because that is where hikers have their great opportunity for recreation, so I am going to speak primarily to the trails aspect. However, I would like to support the National Parks and Conservation Association's testimony. I agree with 95 percent of what Mr. Voorhees said and would certainly support them on what they say.

I would, however, like to put my own personal comments in the record. I have been a long time great supporter and fan of National Parks. I established a goal for myself probably about 20 years ago to try to visit every one of the National Park units. They keep establishing new ones, I am having trouble keeping up, but I have indeed visited well over 200 of the parks, most of those during the last 10 years.

I would like to, from my own personal observations—I am sure this committee knows that there are appalling conditions in the parks. Things are in bad shape, and I have seen a steady decline in the last 10 years of how well things are kept up. The trails are in bad condition, roads are in bad condition, buildings are in bad condition, and, worse of all, the staff are morally depleted, and that is a shame, and I don't blame the staff for that. It is their living conditions and the surroundings they must work in and their low pay scale. So whatever Congress can do to help remedy and restore our sometimes so-called crown jewels to be worthy of that distinction I think would be very worth while.

Primarily on the aspect of trails, I want to support the challenge cost share component of this legislation. Trails are great benefactors of challenge cost share. The trails community has a long time tradition of volunteering to help protect the resources that they love, and trails really do lend themselves well to volunteer efforts. However, it needs support from the Government agencies.

So I think the challenge cost share component that would be fashioned basically after the Forest Service program they developed a few years ago would be very worthwhile. Theirs works well, and, again, I will repeat, trails have been one of the major benefactors of that program.

But I would also like to mention—and this isn't in my written testimony—that we have been, I think, reasonably successful in the last couple of years with developing three-way partnerships through our National Trails Day program where we have an agency cooperator, an organization that supports the trail or a project, and a corporate entity that is cooperating. I think that the corporate entity can provide the funds, the public land management agency can provide the resource, and the people can provide the labor, and I think that is one solution to getting things done without the Government spending a lot more money.

There need to be careful restrictions to make sure that the parks don't become commercialized, I certainly agree with that, and I have heard some concerns about that, but I think partnerships is a way to go to really—especially on trails, to help resolve the sad decline of the conditions in the parks.

Thank you for listening to me today, and I will be happy to answer any questions.

[Prepared statement of Ms. Henley follows:]

AMERICAN HIKING SOCIETY

P.O. Box 20160
Washington, DC 20041-2160
Tel: 703-255-9304
Fax: 703-255-9308

STATEMENT OF: SUSAN A. HENLEY, VICE PRESIDENT
AMERICAN HIKING SOCIETY

PRESENTED TO: THE CONGRESS OF THE UNITED STATES
U.S. HOUSE OF REPRESENTATIVES

COMMITTEE ON NATURAL RESOURCES
SUBCOMMITTEE ON NATIONAL PARKS AND PUBLIC LANDS

June 10, 1994
Subject: H.R. 4533

"National Park Service Entrepreneurial Management Reform Act"

Mr. Chairman and members of the subcommittee:

My name is Susan Henley. I thank you for the opportunity to appear before you today.

The American Hiking Society is an organization that represents the interests of 118 hiking clubs across the nation. Including our individual members we have a combined membership of nearly one-half million hikers. My remarks today will relate mostly to the potential effect that this proposed legislation would have on trails.

However, I also would like to speak from a personal perspective. I have personally visited well over half of this nation's National Parks and National Forests. I have hiked, bicycled, paddled or traveled by horseback in 49 of the 50 states. I am sure the members of this committee are well aware of some of the appalling conditions existing today in most of our once beautiful National Parks. For a number of years these parks have been called the crown jewels of this nation. Unfortunately that can no longer be claimed for all too many of them. During my own personal visits to our parks during the past 40 years, I have witnessed a steady decline in the condition of trails, buildings, roads, and, most disturbing of all, the morale and attitude of the park employees. The employees are not to blame for their morale and attitude, it is certainly justified by their living

Promoting Hiking & Trails in America
243 Church Street, Suite 300-A Vienna, VA 22180

and working surroundings. Something needs to be done soon to restore our crown jewels to be deserving of that destination and of our pride in having outstanding cultural and natural resources protected for future generations.

The American Hiking Society has surveyed the membership of our organization twice during the past 9 years about their willingness to pay user fees. Both times the results were the same. Our members overwhelmingly were willing to pay user fees for resources (see attachments 1 & 2). But most of the respondents wanted strong assurances that the fees collected would be used to maintain the resource that they use. This proposed legislation appears to address that issue considerably better than the current law.

I don't believe there are fees proposed specifically for trails. However if the authority to set fees lay directly with the Secretary, it would be difficult for us to know and monitor the effectiveness. One of our major concerns, on the issue of fees for trails in wilderness and other backcountry areas, is the administrative cost to issue the permits and monitor for violations on the part of users. It just seems nearly impossible to me that the administrative cost would not be greater than the funds collected for some remote areas that are accessible only by trail. There is insufficient research material available to allow members of Congress to debate this issue of administrative cost versus revenue. It seems to me that it would be more useful to collect daily user fees for those locations that have high use of a repetitive nature.

The American Hiking Society fully supports the concept of providing greater opportunities and funding possibilities for Challenge Cost-Share Agreements. Trails have been a major benefactor of the extensive somewhat flexible challenge cost share program developed by the USDA Forest Service a couple of years ago. Members of the trails community have a long standing tradition of volunteering to help to build and maintain the trails on public lands and certainly would welcome this spirit of better cooperation to help with the cost of materials and logistics in support of their volunteer efforts. Let us not overlook the great potential of cooperative management partnerships, such as the highly successful partnerships over the last several years with the Appalachian Trail Conference.

I would be please to answer any questions.

Thanks for the opportunity to speak today regarding this important reform act.

Attachment #1 - AHS Statement on HR 4533

American Hiker

The Official Publication of the American Hiking Society

MAY 1985

Survey

TOTAL SAMPLE of 2,326

		YES	NO
1.	A) Hikers should pay excise taxes on their purchases of hiking equipment.	21%	75%
	B) Hikers should pay fees for use of trails.	37%	59%
2.	IF Congress decides to raise money from hikers, the less objectionable (preferable) choice is:	22%	56%
		EXCISE TAXES	USE FEES
3.	IF Congress legislates excise taxes or use fees, the funds should be spent for:		
	A) trails and backcountry camping;	87%	5%
	B) "non-game" wildlife (as proposed in the *Federal Register*);	47%	34%
	C) management of wilderness areas;	80%	8%
	D) backcountry search and rescue;	51%	30%
	E) all general programs in parks, forests and other public lands;	24%	57%
	F) any federal government expense.	2%	77%
4.	As an alternative to daily use fees, hikers should have an option of purchasing an annual fixed fee trail entry permit, such as the Park Service's Golden Eagle Passport.	85%	13%
5.	Only hikers who cause heavy impacts should be charged use fees—such as hikers who camp overnight, hikers who enter wilderness areas, or hikers who enter fragile geologic or biologic areas.	29%	65%
6.	I would reduce my usage of trails where use fees were charged.	39%	57%
7.	I would reduce the number, quality or frequency of my purchases of equipment if a 5%–10% excise tax were charged.	57%	38%

8. A) During the past 12 months, I hiked trails in ____ (number) states. 1=19%; 2=24%; 3=21%; 4=12%; 5=5%; 6 or more–6%

B) During the past 12 months, the number of days I spent hiking was:

Under 5	5–10	11–25	Over 25
11%	24%	32%	32%

C) My hikes go through federal land

Under 33%	33%–67%	Over 67%
27%	37%	35%

of the time.

AMERICAN HIKING SOCIETY MEMBERSHIP SURVEY

Date: September, 1991

WILLING TO PAY USERS FEES FOR BETTER TRAILS

6. Are you willing to pay user fees to help provide for better trails?

Total answering	100.0%
Yes	80.0%
No	20.0%

Base - 317
N/A - 6

Mrs. MINK. Thank you very much.

Mr. Duncan, do you have any questions?

Mr. DUNCAN. No, I have no questions, thank you.

Mrs. MINK. We appreciate both of your testimony.

I don't know, Mr. Voorhees, that I quite agree with your notion that this broad authority ought to be given to the Park Service. I think that, as you suggested in part of your testimony, there needs to be some very active residual authority in the Congress to review what types of fees and other kinds of revenue efforts are being made by the Park Service.

I do agree with the idea that a larger portion of the revenues ought to be reserved to the parks that generate the revenues for their operational costs.

One part of your testimony Ms. Henley, having to do with volunteer workers: To what extent does the Park Service now, as you have examined, utilize volunteers in their general maintenance and operational activities.

Ms. HENLEY. I don't have any statistics or haven't done any research on this, but my observation in visiting many parks is that the volunteers in the park program are used a great deal for interpreter services.

What I am promoting is that we develop a challenge cost share program that can provide actually more maintenance type projects on trails and other areas rather than just the interpretive services aspect of it. The challenge cost share effectiveness works very well to facilitate that.

Mrs. MINK. Mr. Voorhees, do you have any objection to enlarging the volunteer corps idea with the Park Service?

Mr. VOORHEES. No, Ma'am.

Mrs. MINK. Are you familiar with the extent to which volunteers are currently used in the parks to help them with maintenance and other operational activities?

Mr. VOORHEES. Helping with maintenance, I am not so sure. I would certainly invite those who are left from the Park Service to provide some comment.

Mrs. MINK. Well, I can direct a question to the Park Service, but it seems to me that that is an area for enhanced support because I think the community out there in all of our areas would be very much interested in participating, they just need to have good supervision and guidances to make sure that the appropriate things are being done and not just to send them off into the wilderness.

Mr. VOORHEES. I am well aware that the administration is fully behind a full blown volunteer corps concept, as is the National Park Service individually, but I am not sure that providing a more substantial number of volunteers answers all the problems.

Mrs. MINK. No, not all, but it certainly would be part of this whole scheme of enhancing resource protection responsibility of the Park Service, and it seems to me, at least from what I am aware in my own two parks, not a whole lot of volunteers are being encouraged to participate.

Now that the administration is concentrating on community service and as we debate welfare reform which has again to rely on community service, we ought to think of ways in which this group of individuals can be used to enhance the park activities.

Mr. VOORHEES. I agree completely.

Ms. HENLEY. Could I make another comment on this issue? I have not seen statistics on the dollar value of a challenge cost share or a participating agreement or what-have-you on the Park Service, but I have seen such statistics on the Forest Service and the BLM, and predominantly the value of a volunteer project provides two-to-one the number of dollars that the agency puts into it, so if there is $1 million that goes into that arena, they are likely to get $3 million worth of services out of it. So I think that speaks well for the usefulness of developing a stronger challenge cost share program.

Mrs. MINK. I quite agree, and I think that is something that needs to be explored with the Park Service to understand what is now ongoing and what could be enlarged within their own program authority.

I know with respect to fund-raising, I participated in one such activity with the Kalaupapa National Historic Park in my State. The church which was built by Father Damien had fallen victim to some pretty savage storms and suffered tremendous erosion effects from the fact that the roof leaked and they were not able to repair it, and there were impediments to the Park Service coming in, some citing the religious nature of the entity, which I thought was rather spurious because the church was only used one day a year and it was a part of the Park Service property, but they felt reluctant to go in and make some major repairs, so they called on the community to come in, and we raised about $600,000 to repair that small building.

So I know that private activities can provide substantial support, and if we need to find some ways to institutionalize the method, I think that is appropriate, and certainly nobody went around and put their names on the pews indicating how much money they gave. I mean that was strictly forbidden in the agreement that the Park Service signed with the committee that was organized which I chaired to raise the funds necessary to protect this asset.

So I am fully aware of the potential of private donations, and I would like to see the idea of volunteerism be incorporated in the Park Service plans before aggressive efforts are made to increase the park fees. I am very much concerned about that in my area.

So I appreciate your testimony, and I am sure that the Members will likewise take advantage of your comments, and I thank you very much for coming today to enlarge our perspective.

If there is no further business before the subcommittee, the subcommittee stands adjourned. Thank you.

[Whereupon, at 10:55 a.m., the subcommittee was adjourned.]

APPENDIX

JUNE 10, 1994

ADDITIONAL MATERIAL SUBMITTED FOR THE HEARING RECORD

PATSY T. MINK
SECOND DISTRICT, HAWAII

WASHINGTON OFFICE:
2135 RAYBURN HOUSE OFFICE BUILDING
WASHINGTON, DC 20515-1102
(202) 225-4906
FAX (202) 225-4987

DISTRICT OFFICE:
5104 PRINCE KUHIO FEDERAL BUILDING
P.O. BOX 50124
HONOLULU, HI 96850-4977
(808) 541-1986
FAX (808) 538-0233

Congress of the United States
House of Representatives
Washington, DC 20515-1102

COMMITTEE ON STEERING AND POLICY
COMMITTEE ON BUDGET
COMMITTEE ON EDUCATION AND LABOR
SUBCOMMITTEES:
ELEMENTARY, SECONDARY & VOCATIONAL EDUCATION
POSTSECONDARY EDUCATION
LABOR MANAGEMENT RELATIONS
COMMITTEE ON NATURAL RESOURCES
COMMITTEE ON GOVERNMENT OPERATIONS (on leave)

June 9, 1994

Patsy T. Mink

OPENING STATEMENT
THE HONORABLE PATSY T. MINK
HEARING ON H.R. 4533, PROPOSED PARK FEE CHANGES

Thank you Mr. Chair. I'm glad that we're here to examine the many issues in this important piece of legislation which proposes a number of changes in the National Park System. I agree with efforts which allow the National Park System to better meet its growing demands brought on by a healthy stream of visitors through our nation's recreational areas. However, I cannot help but be wary of possible efforts to increase entrance fees at our park units.

Our country's parks were meant for the use and enjoyment of all Americans. This is why I think that it's dangerous to speak of eliminating current caps on per vehicle and per person entrance fees. It isn't fair, for those in our communities without the financial means to live comfortably, to make it even harder for them to appreciate the natural beauty preserved in parks near their homes, or even parks in parts of the country they have heard of all their lives but cannot even have a chance to peek at. Little Peter will not be able to understand why he has to sit alone in his classroom back at school while his friends whose parents could afford the field trip fee of $4 get to board the bus for a day at the park.

The Honorable Patsy T. Mink

Page 2

Another issue dealing with fees of concern to me, which I hope Director Roger Kennedy will address during his testimony today, is that I understand the Park Service is considering a possible elimination of current per vehicle entrance fees. I see this as conceivably detrimental to the future of our parks, as the assessment of these fees encourages visitors to carpool and cut down on the numbers of cars which enter the parks. We need no growth in the demand for road maintenance in these areas. It's also important to reduce as much as possible the damage caused to the plant and animal life in the parks, which is already disturbed by our presence.

Finally, I would like to address reservations I have about the proposed establishment of the National Park Renewal Fund. Through H.R. 4533, half of all new recreation fees would be funnelled into this new fund, beginning in Fiscal Year 1996, and distributed to collecting and non-collecting parks. I understand that the Park Service cannot fully account for its current distribution of user fees as mandated by current law: 10% by the Director based on need, 40% to all units for operating costs and 50% to collecting parks based on amount of collection. I would like to caution that if current revenue distribution mandates cannot be met, the Park Service should take the effort to come up to speed with these requirements before creating a new and similar system for entrance fees. Thank you, Mr. Chair.

STATEMENT OF
THE HONORABLE JAMES V. HANSEN
ON H.R. 4533
JUNE 10, 1994

Mr. Chairman, I guess what we are all about today is money. Money for our parks. As I said in the article I prepared for Roll Call several months ago, I think the lack of funding, along with designation of parks of questionable merit, are the two biggest problems facing the National Park Service today. Thanks to your involvement Mr. Chairman, I believe we are on our way toward addressing that latter issue in a bi-partisan fashion.

Money will be a tougher issue to solve. It appears to me that there are two choices for funding, we can either get money from users and activities which take place at parks, or we can take it from taxpayers at large. Right now, park users pay a total of about $94 million annually or about 7 cents of every dollar it costs to run the parks, and the taxpayers at large pay the remaining 93 cents.

Mr. Chairman, that is not the proper balance. As I have stated in the past, recreational use of Federal lands is the most subsidized use of Federal lands, subsidized to the tune of $1.3 billion this year. That subsidy should be reduced.

So how do we close that funding gap? The Administration endorses a bill which according to CBO will provide no increase in funding from concession fees and presents us with a bill to generate only about $36 million in user fees. However, in the last year, this same Administration has endorsed legislation to spend $35 million annually on heritage areas, $25 million annually on the Presidio and $10 million annually on California Desert legislation. Mr. Chairman, we are quite clearly widening this funding shortfall gap, not closing it.

I am not opposed to this bill per se, over a year ago I offered an amendment to the Budget Act which incorporated the substantive revenue generating provisions of this measure. In fact, my proposal would have raised 3 times as much new fee revenue as the measure before us today. As you may recall, my amendment was defeated on a straight party line vote. However, considering everyone's great desire to expand the park system, even that proposal was not enough.

In closing, Mr. Chairman, let me just state I recognize the magnitude of the funding problem facing the National Park Service, and I would hope we could work on a bi-partisan basis to find real solutions, just as we cooperated on the National Park Service Reform bill.

STATEMENT OF THE HONORABLE TIM JOHNSON

HEARING ON HR 4533

SUBCOMMITTEE OF NATIONAL PARKS, FORESTS, AND PUBLIC LANDS

CHAIRMAN BRUCE VENTO

JUNE 10, 1994

Mr. Chairman, I am looking forward to reviewing the testimony presented to the Subcommittee today on HR 4533, the National Park Service Entrepreneurial Management Reform Act. I certainly can appreciate the fact that each year it becomes increasingly difficult for the Park Service to maintain and operate our nation's parks with the limited resources available. I am also fully aware that under the current budget climate and the need to reduce the federal budget deficit, it is unlikely the Park Service will see an increase in the appropriations needed to reduce the backlog of physical needs throughout the Park system.

However, the issue of visitor fees is currently prohibited by law for some of our most cherished Park Service units, including Mount Rushmore in my home state of South Dakota. As the only member of the US House of Representatives for South Dakota, I am concerned about the message the Congress will send if it allows the Park Service to charge citizens to see some of our country's most recognized symbols of democracy, as well as the possible negative economic impacts of an entrance fee to Mt. Rushmore. One provision in HR 4533 which I think moves park policy in the right direction would allow for the collecting park to keep a greater portion of revenues collected. These revenues could then be used for some of the much needed maintenance and repair work at many of our park facilities. As we all know, the issue of user fees is an extremely salient one, and I will be interested to hear the reactions of my constituents to the proposed legislation and the statements made here this morning.

I think today's hearing and discussion will be a good starting point for dialogue on this measure, and I appreciate the witnesses taking the time to come and share their thoughts with us this morning. Thank you Mr. Chairman for an opportunity to comment on this issue today.

OPENING STATEMENT
OF
THE HONORABLE JAY DICKEY
Fourth District - Arkansas
Before the
NATIONAL PARKS, FORESTS, AND PUBLIC LANDS SUBCOMMITTEE
Regarding
H.R. 4533 - Entrepreneurial Management of the National Park Service

June 10, 1994

Mr. Chairman, thanks for holding this hearing on H.R. 4533, as proposed by the Administration.

I've been calling here for more investment in the much needed construction and repair backlogs at units of the National Park System, before we add new units. I've especially focused on much needed rehabilitation to the Historic Landmark Bathhouse Row at Hot Springs National Park. Director Kennedy and I have had previous conversations about this.

So, while I support additional funding for these purposes, I don't see how this bill responds in a meaningful way. As I understand it, under the bill, only half of the increased fees collected will go into a Park Restoration Fund, and the other half goes to deficit reduction, not to the Park Service. While I firmly support deficit reduction, we also have to address in a meaningful manner, the National Park Service enormous construction and repair deficit. This bill does not do that in a significant way. The annual expected revenue increase from these entrance and recreation fee increases are more than wiped out by several new units to the National Park System that have already been reported out of the Natural Resources Committee.

I look forward to the testimony. Maybe my views can be changed. But, it seems to me we need to find a better way to address this funding problem, obviously through the appropriations process, without further burdening visitors who already pay to visit our National Parks.

Thank you.

ORCA

Outdoor Recreation Coalition of America

303-444-3353
Fax: 444-3284
P.O. Box 1319
Boulder, CO
80306

August 1, 1994

The Honorable Bruce Vento
U.S. House of Representatives
Washington, DC 20515

Dear Congressman Vento:

The Outdoor Recreation Coalition of America (ORCA) represents a diverse cross-section of interests in human-powered outdoor recreation.

ORCA's Legislative Affairs Committee has been following the progress of the National Park Service Entrepreneurial Management Reform Act, which you introduced, to determine its potential benefits to outdoor recreation.

Based on our knowledge of the bill, ORCA has chosen to support the National Park Service Entrepreneurial Management Reform Act subject to the considerations detailed below.

ORCA supports giving the Secretary of the Interior the discretion to set reasonable and prudent fees for park entrance, and for user activities, and for the Golden Eagle Passport. ORCA also supports allowing the National Park Service (NPS) to set prices for annual passes for individual or regional groups of park(s). Placing this authority with the Department of Interior (DOI) and with the NPS more readily ensures fees will be assessed based on the needs of the Park System as opposed to political considerations but we would not object to the concept of joint authority between DOI and Congress.

ORCA will withdraw its support if fees become unreasonably high or serve to limit the access of the economically disadvantaged, or if fees concentrate on a specific user group to the exclusion of others. For this reason, ORCA would approve of raising the cap without withdrawing it entirely. Additionally, ORCA believes that the authority to collect fees can only be justified when the associated costs of administration can be held to a proportionate level.

ORCA is in favor of revenues collected by the NPS being returned to the NPS budget to create a National Park Renewal Fund. ORCA believes that user fees should always contribute to the resource the users pay for. While a guarantee of 50% is an improvement over the current situation, ORCA would support the designation of an even higher percentage of the fees collected as not subject to other appropriations. It is also essential the revenues collected from park users **supplement** NPS budgets. **The Renewal Fund must not replace allocations from the general fund.**

ORCA believes it is important to state that user fees can only be expected to cover a portion of the budgets of federal land agencies. Specifically, user fees could provide revenues for operation and maintenance but capital expenditures for such things as land acquisition must be funded by alternative sources.

The distribution of 50% of the Renewal Fund money to the collecting park and 50% for specific projects is appropriate. It would fairly balance funding between highly used parks and high priority projects.

For these reasons, based on these conditions, ORCA supports the National Park Service Entrepreneurial Management Reform Act.

Sincerely,

David Secunda
Executive Director

cc: Secretary Bruce Babbit

Travel and Tourism Government Affairs Council
1100 New York Avenue, NW
Suite 450
Washington, DC 20005-3934
202-408-9600
FAX 202-408-1255

July 29, 1994

The Honorable Bruce F. Vento
Chairman
Subcommittee on National Parks, Forests and Public Lands
Committee on Natural Resources
United States House of Representatives
Washington, DC 20515

Re: **H.R. 4533**

Dear Mr. Chairman:

The Travel and Tourism Government Affairs Council takes this opportunity to express its support for H.R. 4533, the "National Park Service Entrepreneurial Management Reform Act", as amended by the subcommittee. The Travel and Tourism Government Affairs Council is the national organization that represents the position of the unified travel and tourism industry on legislative and regulatory issues of common concern, and is comprised of thirty-six major national travel and tourism organizations, as well as twelve at-large corporate executives, representing every segment of this $6 billion industry. We commend you personally, Mr. Chairman, for your initiative and vision in introducing H.R. 4533.

As our industry depends on the promotion and encouragement of convenient and enjoyable travel and tourism opportunities, we recognize the need to ensure that the highest quality services are provided by top travel and tourism destinations and attractions. America's national parks are just such attractions, and continue to be among this nation's popular tourist sites. In order for these majestic treasures to remain as such, adequate funding must be obtained to ensure their upkeep and continuation.

With this in mind, the Council supports the subcommittee's substitute version of H.R. 4533, particularly the provision requiring that 100 percent of funds in excess of collection costs be deposited in the "National Park Renewal Fund". We believe it is imperative that these collected funds then be available without appropriation for park use. We also support the provision which would retain Congressional authority to set fees.

Thank you for your consideration of the Council's views concerning this legislation.

Sincerely,

Aubrey C. King
Executive Director

American Automobile Association

Washington Office

1440 New York Avenue, N.W.
Suite 200
Washington, D.C. 20005
202/942-2050

FAX 202/783-4788

Darryl L. Wyland
Senior Vice President
Public & Government Relations

June 29, 1994

The Honorable Bruce F. Vento
Chairman
Subcommittee on National Parks, Forests
and Public Lands
Committee on Natural Resources
United States House of Representatives
Washington, D.C. 20515

Dear Mr. Chairman:

The American Automobile Association appreciates this opportunity to submit our views on H.R. 4533, the "National Park Service Entrepreneurial Management Reform Act." We respectfully request that this written statement be included in the official record of the Subcommittee's 10 June 1994 hearing.

AAA is a not-for-profit federation of 127 motor clubs serving nearly 36 million members in the United States and Canada. Among the many services provided AAA members are travel services, including maps, TripTiks, TourBooks, CampBooks, and other specialized travel publications. Our members rely upon AAA for accurate, useful, and reliable travel information.

Many AAA members travel to this country's national parks every year. In fact, sites managed by the National Park System consistently rank among the top five destinations for AAA members. The popularity of the national parks among AAA members is accompanied by their increasing concern about the deterioration in park maintenance and services and the wear and tear on park lands.

Reflecting this strong AAA member interest in enjoying the nation's national park treasures while protecting and conserving federal lands for future generations, AAA policy supports federal, state, and local government efforts promoting the protection, conservation, and prudent use of our natural resources for recreational purposes.

AAA policy "endorses reasonable user fees for recreational use of federal lands **if the fees are used to maintain and protect the lands from which they were collected**" (Emphasis added).

AAA believes H.R. 4533 is a good beginning toward reflecting AAA policy of providing for national park needs through user fees. In particular, we endorse the concept embodied in Section 4(d)(3) under which 50 percent of the additional fee receipts would be deposited in a "National Park Renewal Fund" to be available **without appropriation** for park needs.

This concept of returning user fees directly to the parks without going through the budget process is extremely important to AAA's support for park user fees. In fact, our support for expanded user fees is expressly conditioned upon the requirement that park user fees not be treated as general funds subject to appropriation. AAA members will support paying reasonable fees to visit the national parks, but only if they know their money is going to be used for park needs. Their support for admission fees evaporates quickly and irrevocably if the fees are to be paid into the general Treasury for deficit reduction or other general fund purposes.

Therefore, AAA urges the Subcommittee not only to endorse the concept of the National Park Renewal Fund as proposed in Section 4, but to amend it to require that all additional receipts collected be deposited in that fund and be available, without further appropriation, for park needs. Any other disposition of national park admission fees would destroy support for such fees and deprive the national parks of a legitimate funding source.

AAA has some concerns with the bill's proposal in Section 4(1) that the Secretary of the Interior establish reasonable admission fees. Our understanding is that this language would permit the Secretary to set fees without even a requirement for public comment. AAA firmly believes public input should be required before fees are imposed. We therefore suggest that, at the very least, proposed fees be published in the Federal Register for public comment.

AAA is interested in working with the Subcommittee and with the National Park Service in crafting legislation that assesses fair and reasonable fees upon users of the national parks. As we stated earlier, however, AAA **cannot** support fees which are paid into the general Treasury for appropriation rather than being available directly to the parks for infrastructure, maintenance, and conservation uses.

I appreciate this opportunity to submit AAA's views on H.R. 4533 and look forward to working with you on this important issue.

Very truly yours,

Darryl L Wyland

Darryl L. Wyland

Conference of National Park Cooperating Associations

June 14, 1994

The Honorable Bruce Vento
Chairman
Subcommittee on National Parks, Forests and Public Lands
812 O'Neil House Office Building
Washington D.C. 20515

Re: H.R. 4533 NPS Entrepreneurial Management Reform Act

Dear Chairman Vento:

On behalf of the Conference of National Park Cooperating Associations I request that this letter be entered into the hearing record for HR 4533, The National Park Service Entrepreneurial Management Reform Act.

The Conference of National Park Cooperating Associations (CNPCA) is the umbrella organization for over sixty Congressionally chartered non-profit/tax exempt interpretive associations operating bookstores and sales areas in our 365 national parks as well as in other federal, state and municipal visitor centers. Since 1920 cooperating associations have worked in partnership with the National Park Service and to date they have contributed aid totaling more than $100 million dollars to the national parks. Each year our member associations continue to contribute about $15 million in support of a variety of National Park Service sanctioned educational programs, visitor services and research activities in our nation's parks.

Collectively the national park cooperating associations are the single largest contributors of financial support to the National Park System. The Conference of National Park Cooperating Associations would like to go on record supporting those sections of H.R. 4533 that provide expanded authority to the National Park Service for the purpose of collecting higher levels of entrance and user fees and to enhance the Service's "partnership" authorities. We are particularly supportive of provisions that would enable the Service to negotiate and enter into cost-share agreements with a wide range of "cooperators." We do have concerns, however, about the provision in this legislation that would establish guidelines for a special permit system to recover not just costs relating to administration of a special use permit, but also would permit the NPS to charge fees on a "value basis" to park users.

CNB Plaza · Suite 302
200 Forks of the River Parkway
Sevierville, TN 37862
615 · 428 · 4239

CNPCA strongly supports the suggested revision to the challenge cost-share program. Cooperating associations have a wide range of opportunities to facilitate fundraising in the parks and cost-sharing is one such tool. Enacting this provision would enable the Secretary of the Interior to enter into cost-share agreements with the cooperating associations, other interpretive associations, "Friends of" groups, and a wide range of other organizations working to enhance the quality of national park programs. We whole-heartedly support the language in Section 6 of this proposed legislation.

The June 10 hearing on this legislation prompted considerable discussion on the collection and retention of fees collected from certain categories of special park users. Specifically, the National Park Service would like to collect not just "administrative costs," but also "fair market value" fees from entities that wish to, for example, film park resources for the production of movies and videos. Such a provision would hamper the efforts of a variety of non-profit entities including production companies affiliated with Public Television stations, colleges and universities, educational institutions and other non-profit organizations with an "agency relation" to the National Park Service from advancing both their own and NPS's educational mission. For example, several non-profit cooperating associations and Friends-of groups have produced park videos that are sold in the parks; the revenue generated is returned to the parks, often in the form of a cash donation. If cooperating associations are charged the same rate as commercial film companies for access to park resources, the additional production costs could make the film project unviable. The imposition of such fees would detrimentally impact the donation levels the associations would be able to give back to the NPS.

Clearly, a special exemption provision is needed to exclude the application of a "value fee" for park users with an educational mission, and for official NPS "cooperators" that have an agency relation with the Service. These groups should pay only a reasonable fee designed to reimburse the NPS for actual incurred expenses during a special event or as a consequence of another sanctioned special use. We urge you to amend this legislation to specifically exclude the payment of a "market value" fee for non-profit organizations, educational institutions and organizations that have an agency relation with the National Park Service.

Thank you for addressing our concerns with respect to this legislation. Should you have any questions or special concerns relating to our position, please do not hesitate to contact me.

Sincerely,

Bruce Craig
Executive Director

○